WOM AND GE WOR NYMPHOMANIA

Theodora, a young exhibitionist, enjoyed going on picnics with ten or more virile young men—with one purpose in mind.

Queen Zingua of Angola, a seventeenth century ruler, kept a harem of males. Her hobby: arranging battles to the death between two of them, then sleeping with the winner.

Julia, a bride for the second time at 18, also had dozens of boys and men as lovers. No desire—however grotesque—went unfulfilled.

Catherine the Great, Empress of Russia, reveled in every heterosexual and homosexual excess. In her old age, she delighted in attending orgies.

The nymphomaniac—no matter what her era or role in life—always has been scorned and rejected by society. In this book, the documented facts reveal the full and intimate details of her problem.

NYMPHOMANIA

A Study of
The Oversexed Woman

Dr. Albert Ellis
and
Edward Sagarin

MB

A MACFADDEN-BARTELL BOOK

THIS BOOK IS THE COMPLETE TEXT
OF THE HARDCOVER EDITION

A MACFADDEN BOOK 1965

MACFADDEN BOOKS are published by
Macfadden-Bartell Corporation
205 East 42nd Street, New York, New York, 10017

Library of Congress Catalog Card Number: 64-12406

Detailed information about the works referred to in this study
will be found in the references following the final chapter. In
the text, references are identified by author's name and date of
publication, in parentheses.

TABLE OF CONTENTS

Author's Note

This book is a collaboration, and the two authors accept responsibility for all statements in it. However, because one of the authors is a clinical psychologist and psychotherapist, when the first person singular is used, it is Dr. Ellis who is speaking.

For the material in this work, the authors have drawn upon many case histories. Not one of the cases concerns a single person. They are all composites and are presented in this way to preserve the anonymity of the people involved. No person is named or described.

THE AUTHORS

Introduction

ALTHOUGH HUNDREDS OF VOLUMES AND MILLIONS OF words are written today on almost every aspect of sex, the peculiar problems of the promiscuous woman are little discussed—and even less understood. She is a popular subject of superficial conversation, the butt of bawdy jokes, and the object of wish-fulfilling fantasies. But few have stopped to consider whether there *is* such a person as an oversexed woman and, if so, how frequently she is encountered, and whether her condition will respond to treatment.

Although recent data has been utilized in studies of many sex practices, there has thus far been little application of this information to the realm of nymphomania. It is our hope that in making this information available, and subjecting it to critical analysis, the understanding of the several forms of female hypersexuality will be enhanced.

Many men dream of finding a "nymphomaniac," and look upon her as a boon, but what they are actually thinking of is an easy-to-seduce woman—*not* a nymphomaniac. The seduction of a male by a compulsive woman (with whose emotional disturbances he is in no way prepared to cope) can be a serious problem to *him*.

An understanding of the causes of nymphomania can lead to an adjustment of negative social attitudes and prejudices that cause society to castigate unfairly the compulsively promiscuous woman and to induce her, needlessly, to self-blame. Knowledge in depth about this problem may afford general insight into related sexual difficulties: frigidity, masochism and other disturbances.

The peculiarly ambivalent attitude of our society toward highly sexed women, who are both celebrated and scorned, is particularly demonstrated in the study of nymphomania. By investigating female hypersexuality and its societal ramifications, we hope to bring to light current sexual attitudes—the divergence between man's actual and his alleged activities, between his laws and the social realities. We may then see some of the disastrous effects of this contradiction.

PART ONE

Background

1

Nymphomania:
A Definition

ELOISE R.

WHEN I FIRST SAW HER, ELOISE WAS A GOOD-LOOKING, college-educated girl of twenty-two. Married and divorced, she now contemplated a second marriage with a personable young man. But, secretly, she was having sexual relations with a number of other men. Eloise said she wanted to be sure she was really capable of fulfillment.

With her first husband, she had never achieved orgasm; with all the other men, she had reached sexual climax only once. It was on a night when she had been drinking a good deal, and found herself in the company of an uncouth man she would normally have spurned, out on bail because of his alleged participation in an armed robbery. (Despite her frequent change of sex partners, Eloise overflowed with middle-class respectability.)

Every other time, Eloise had failed to have an orgasm. How could she consider marriage again until she knew whether or not she would be constantly frustrated, whether her sexual failure would not bring the planned second marriage to an early end?

In Eloise's case, as in the case of any supposedly frigid woman, I had to determine the extent of frigidity. It seemed at first that she never achieved orgasm. But on further questioning, I discovered that the only technique Eloise would permit was sexual intercourse with the male surmounting her.

11

She would allow a mild degree of preliminary kissing and petting, even though she found this somewhat distasteful. Then, as soon as possible, Eloise would have the man mount her for penile-vaginal copulation. She managed to achieve a mild degree of excitement. But only on that one occasion, after she had been drinking, had she been able to have an orgasm. Even then she wasn't too clear on what actually took place, I learned when I questioned her closely, as to their sexual interplay.

The more I spoke with Eloise, the clearer it became to me that she probably had experienced clitoral manipulation that evening. When sober, Eloise would not permit clitoral stimulation or any other type of extravaginal relations. But on that one occasion, apparently because she was intoxicated and her lover was a person who could not be controlled, she had permitted him to do what he liked. Entering her vagina from the rear, he had massaged her clitoris while they actively copulated, and on this one occasion she had come to climax.

In other instances, when males had tried to arouse Eloise through direct stimulation of the clitoral area, she had steadfastly refused. She considered extravaginal sexuality improper. A woman, she declared, was meant to have orgasm only through "normal" intercourse. If a girl allowed herself to make love in other ways, oral intercourse, for example, or if she permitted digital manipulation, she was a "pervert." Such were Eloise's fixed ideas.

Actively and forthrightly, I began to discuss with Eloise her notions about sex. The idea that only straight intercourse is proper, I showed her, is basically a religious taboo originating thousands of years ago among ancient peoples largely interested in procreation rather than in sexual pleasure. Other groups, among them several Oriental peoples, have no such taboos and think nothing of having a variety of relations, usually, though not necessarily, ending with penile-vaginal copulation. Among these groups women tend to have orgasms more frequently and more intensely than women who engage only in regular intercourse.

I also explained to Eloise that, anatomically, it made no sense for some females to have straight intercourse and expect to have an orgasm. For, as has recently been shown, in unusually good research by William H. Masters and Virginia Johnson of the Department of Gynecology of Washington University Medical School in St. Louis (Johnson and Masters, 1962; Master and Johnson, 1961, 1962), the female orgasm normally results indirectly, if not directly, from clitoral stimulation. Masters and Johnson discovered by observing

12

females as they were actually undergoing orgasm that when the female obtains a climax through intercourse, she does so because the inner lips of the genitalia penetrate sufficiently into the entrance of the vagina. These inner lips are stimulated by the base of the penis during intercourse. When this occurs and when these inner lips of the female pull rhythmically on the clitoral region, orgasm ensues.

In those cases where the inner lips are not extensive enough to enter the vaginal area, or where the penis does not pull properly on them, or where they are not connected adequately with the clitoral region, the female will almost never receive orgasm from intercourse alone. Even when females are adequately equipped, when their labia reach into the vaginal area and pull rhythmically on the clitoral region during coitus, they still may only receive orgasm on a limited number of occasions.

However, when the clitoral region is directly stimulated, by the woman or by the fingers or tongue of the male partner, she can achieve orgasm almost every time. This is the basic observation which the Kinsey investigators made years ago. They showed that the average female is capable of orgasm 95 per cent of the time *if* she is properly aroused —particularly when her inner lips and clitoral region are adequately stimulated in a rhythmic manner.

I explained these scientific facts to Eloise, indicating that there is no reason why the average woman should obtain orgasm only through penile-vaginal copulation. Many women, of course, *do* regularly achieve orgasm in this manner. But there are millions of females who virtually never reach orgasm by penile-vaginal stimulation alone, *and there is no reason to believe that these women are biologically or otherwise abnormal.* When these women do obtain orgasm, usually by direct clitoral stimulation, then, as Masters and Johnson have shown, their orgasms are exactly the same, anatomically and physiologically, as those achieved by women who experience orgasm during penile-vaginal copulation.

This does not mean there are no advantages to be obtained through penile-vaginal intercourse. Among other things, the muscles of the vagina tend to respond rhythmically during orgasm. If there is a penis (or a finger) inserted in the vagina at this time, then the women may find greater satisfaction than if she obtained a clitoral orgasm with nothing inserted. Also, as other sexologists have shown for a good many years, the penis pushing the cervix or other parts of the female anatomy during intromission may improve orgasm (Le Mon Clark, 1961).

So, there is nothing wrong with a woman obtaining an orgasm during intercourse; frequently this is a desirable state of affairs. But a desideratum, as I keep stressing to my nonsexually disturbed, as well as to my sexually disturbed patients, is not a necessity. A desired thing is something that we would *preferably* have, but we don't absolutely *need*. And to *make* a desideratum into a necessity is one essence of emotional disturbance.

I explained to Eloise, in no uncertain terms, that although it might be desirable for her to achieve orgasm during intercourse, it was not necessary. Failure did not prove she was abnormal. However, the fact that she never invited non-penile clitoral stimulation showed there was something wrong ideologically. Eloise had clear-cut emotional sex blocks. The answer was to work on these blocks, change her antisexual assumptions, and to have her accept the broader, wiser assumption that orgasm is orgasm, however obtained. I advised her to try everything possible to achieve climax.

At first, Eloise resisted these facts and suggestions. She was horrified at the idea of her fiancé manipulating her clitoris. She contended this was an unpleasant sensation, that it created soreness. But on further investigation, after I induced her to experiment, Eloise discovered that almost all the unpleasantness attributed to clitoral stimulation was really in her mind. She had not *allowed* this act to be anything but unpleasant.

Finally, Eloise found that not only could she have an orgasm, but she would have an ecstatic one each time she did the proper thing. This, in her case, turned out to be manipulation of the clitoral area and of the inner lips. Eloise told me her inner lips were exquisitely sensitive. When either she or her boyfriend stroked them correctly, she invariably reached an explosive orgasm.

What is more, Eloise found (as do most women, according to Masters and Johnson) that if she had one orgasm and then rested a while, she could have two, three, four or more orgasms. Sometimes the third or fourth climax was even more enjoyable than the earlier ones.

After a few weeks of broadening her sexual activities, Eloise discovered she was able to achieve orgasms in different ways, particularly by manipulation of her inner labia.

Once she began to achieve orgasms with her fiancé, Eloise lost most of her inclination to have sexual relations elsewhere. She deliberately experimented with several male partners to see if what was successful with her fiancé would also work with them. She found it did work. Eloise had no

14

difficulty obtaining orgasm with other men. But she also discovered that in the emotional overtones and in the nonsexual relations she had with these other men, her *total* satisfaction was eminently less. She acknowledged, although she had managed to keep this out of her consciousness before, that it was risky to have sex relations with other men because her fiancé was certain to find out, no matter how discreet she was.

Thus, Eloise voluntarily gave up sex relations with men other than her fiancé. She also discovered, after a few more weeks, that relations with her fiancé continued to improve until they reached a peak of satisfaction she thought almost incredible.

By this time, her nymphomania was at an end. Eloise had no incentive for compulsive promiscuity. She still admired other men, considered them attractive, but had no serious interest in them. Eloise, to her own surprise, had become completely monogamous.

When I last saw Eloise, a few weeks after she married her fiancé, they were getting along splendidly. I recommended further therapy, to clear up some of her nonsexual difficulties, but she decided against this. While I doubt that Eloise is a *perfectly* well-adjusted girl, there is no question that her nymphomaniacal tendencies have gone and that she has been able to make a good sexual adjustment to marriage.

The Case of Susan: Is This How It Begins?

Susan was fifteen years old when I first saw her at the New Jersey State Diagnostic Center, where I was Chief Psychologist. She sat opposite me, frightened, emotionally disturbed, and branded a delinquent. A more pathetic child of fifteen would be hard to imagine: underdeveloped, she looked only eleven or twelve, her plain face and unattractive straight hair giving her an air of sexlessness. Yet, she had already had unusual sexual experience. Without psychiatric help, she would drag herself through a life of joyless promiscuity. Susan could not even offer the pretense and bravado of the flirtatious delinquent. She looked at the floor and answered my quesions in monosyllables, if at all.

Susan had been placed in a police shelter after having had sex relations with seven boys on the same day—with only a few moments' rest between partners.

Prior to her induction into the world of sex, Susan had led a generally uneventful life. She did poorly at school, and was unhappy about the constant criticism she received from her

15

parents. Her father, as far as could be determined, was a borderline schizophrenic who went from one small job to another when he did work, drank a good deal, and showed little interest in his children. He was not in the least companionable, and had no hesitation in venting his displeasure on Susan and her younger brother. The mother was an angry and disappointed woman whose negative attitude toward life permeated her existence. Repeatedly, she told Susan she was stupid, uninteresting, ugly, and would never be able to win and hold a boy. The girl's reaction was to go off in a corner and sulk, or she would turn to her romance magazines and comic books.

Susan was capable of handling school work, but usually could not apply herself. Whenever she became disturbed, she immediately gave up.

Typical of those with feelings of inadequacy, she had no friends her own age; she did have several who were younger. She seldom had dates, but spent hours dreaming of a perfect lover who would carry her off to marriage and a life of love.

A few days before her arrest, Susan had become agitated. Instead of going to school that day, she had decided to travel to a nearby city and spend the afternoon at the movies. She took a bus to the city, then wandered aimlessly about, staring in store windows while she waited for the motion picture theatre to open. At some point, a forty-year-old man approached her, struck up a conversation and invited her to his place for a meal. *Why not,* she thought, and in trusting simplicity went along. The man spoke to her in a kindly, interested tone and told her what a pretty girl she was. Then he brought his body close to hers. She received him with little physical response, but she was delighted at his interest.

Susan did not enjoy the ensuing first intercourse. In fact, she found it painful. After it was over, the man held her in his arms, and talked to her about his plans for both of them, plans that meant she could leave school and live with him.

Next day, before going to work, the man urged Susan to go home, promising he would see her again the following weekend.

But Susan was frightened and would not go home. So, again she wandered. Looking lonely and forlorn, she must have been an obvious target for a man on the prowl. This time it was a youth in his early twenties who took her to the movies, then to eat. He too "spoke nicely" to her. They went to his shack on the outskirts of town, and there he lost little time repeating the events of the previous night. He showed her many ways in which their bodies could make contact

16

—and Susan found the acts neither pleasant nor repulsive. She was, in fact, almost indifferent, but if this was what a "kind and sweet guy" liked, she decided she would go along.

The thing that pleased Susan was that she had discovered a method for attracting males. Henceforth, men would show interest in her, and help her.

For three days and three nights Susan lived with the young man. He took care of her, talked to her, cuddled her—and copulated with her, she recalled, about three or four times a day. For a while they were confined to extravaginal play, but after she had healed following her earlier experiences they had intercourse. Again, Susan obtained little enjoyment. But when he caressed every part of her body, she got a good deal of satisfaction, and clung to him. With his arms around her, Susan told me, she felt she was loved and protected.

The young man, in the meantime, boasted to his friends about the girl who was willing to do anything as long as she received a few kindly embraces. Several of them wanted to share her. Believing Susan was more interested in him than in sex, the young man told her to indulge with his friends. He assured her they would be as friendly as he had been. Primarily interested in keeping him, Susan feared if she did not agree to the suggestion, he would leave her. Afraid to return to her parents (and the school authorities), and anxious to please the youth, she consented.

One afternoon Susan's lover brought along seven other boys approximately his own age. For the next few hours, in rapid succession, Susan and a young man would go into the shack. About all that can be said for what ensued is: the young man had sexual intercourse—and Susan did all she could to help. She was, essentially, out of it. Various acts occurred: intercourse in most instances, oral relations in others, and in one case anal relations. She focused on how pleased her lover would be when she was finished.

As it happened, some of the boys talked in a bar that night, and a woman who overheard them notified the police. Subsequently, Susan was taken into custody. As the events unravelled, the authorities believed they were confronted with a youthful case of incipient nymphomania.

Nymphomania is probably the most misused sexual term in the English language. In the last decade or two, sex novels (especially paperbacks), movie ads, and feature articles in men's magazines, have used this term so frequently that it and its diminutive, *nympho,* have become ubiquitous in the sex literature. Almost every villianess of stage, screen, and

17

pulpdom would appear to be a nymphomaniac these days.

The sad part of all this is that there are at least two major misconceptions involved in the use of the term *nymphomania*. First of all, it does *not* merely signify a highly desirous female frequently on the lookout for a male partner. The word has a more precise meaning.

One dictionary defines it in a manner that can be used here as a point of departure: "Morbid and uncontrollable sexual desire in women." One writer, (Clifford Allen, 1962), refers to it as "an illness which may be due to both physical and mental conditions," and describes it as "sexual hyperversion." *Real Life Guide* (1962) has noted that the *nymphomaniac* and the *promiscuous woman* have a great deal in common: 'each drifts from one man to another ... and neither seems to have the ability or the desire to say 'no.' " But the two women are not at all the same, the editor maintains, in an oft-repeated contention which we do *not* find acceptable: "The fundamental difference is that the promiscuous woman may be able to experience an orgasm, where the nymphomaniac cannot."

The second favorite misconception that exists in regard to the highly sexed females rampantly portrayed in modern fiction and drama, *and erroneously called nymphomaniacs,* is that they are in every neighborhood, office, and social gathering, and that all they are interested in is getting a man—preferably some other woman's man—into bed as quickly as possible. What claptrap!

As Kinsey and his associates clearly showed, only about two per cent of American women equal or surpass the erotic excitability of the average male. Most of these women are, in spite of their unusually high degree of sexual interest, distinctly restrained in their activities.

Women—although wishful-thinking males prefer to believe otherwise—are seldom primarily motivated by unrestrained libido. They are mainly absorbed in matters of love, marriage, and child-rearing, rather than of pure sexuality. And they will usually copulate or not copulate in direct relation to how they feel about their male partner—how emotionally attached they are to him, and think he is to them. No matter how much they are physically motivated, they will hold back if they suspect that he, or mama, or "people," will disapprove.

The picture, then, of the typical twenty-year-old nymphomaniac who, upon her first meeting with handsome Bob, playfully attacks him, is utter hogwash. Even if she *felt* like doing so, the chances are she wouldn't. What she really feels, in most instances, is that *he* should love *her* madly—and love her *in spite of* rather than because of her sexiness. For even the highly sexed girl wants to be loved primarily *for herself.*

The term nymphomania has become an epithet, hurled by the self-righteous against all females whose sexual activities do not follow the patterns laid down by society. Males who are strong protectors of the double standard, who envy and admire the Don Juan, cast this term of contempt at the woman who makes herself easily available—even as they seek to seduce her.

Discussion of nymphomania in serious literature is seldom encountered. In the two-volume *Encyclopedia of Sexual Behavior* (Ellis and Abarbanel, 1961) the word appears but once; a sign that the authors may have shunned the word as being unscientific, or that the condition that it depicts is so infrequently met that it does not deserve a serious place in the literature of sexual anomalies. Early writers, who occasionally described a case of uncontrollable sexuality in a woman, used such terms as hypersexuality, erotomania and urethromania. The last two of these terms were especially applied to women who would fit the definition of *true* nymphomania.

Promiscuity is One Thing; Nymphomania, Another

Nymphomania, in its *true* form, is a rare condition, and although it has many elements in common with promiscuity, the two states have quite different causes and effects.

What is often termed nymphomania is *usually* promiscuity, relatively well controlled, probably highly selective, and of a nature that would be considered relatively normal if found in almost any male in our society. Aside from their having several lovers, the promiscuous woman and the nymphomaniac have little in common.

These are the characteristics of nymphomania:

1. Lack of Control. A nymphomaniac's desires are uncontrollable. They refuse to be contained within a rational scheme of living, in which sexual fulfillment is wisely sought and obtained. When her urges arise, they must quickly be fulfilled, even if the consequences of fulfillment are likely to be serious.

Nymphomania, in this respect, can best be understood by comparison with other uncontrollable urges that grip

19

some human beings: to eat specific foods, to smoke, to overindulge in alcohol, or to bathe excessively.

With nymphomania, unlike the controlled and selective promiscuity that characterizes a sizable portion of American womanhood (Anthony, 1962), friendships and family relationship can be damaged, work can be sacrificed; for in nymphomania there is no time but the present and no man but the one you're with.

2. *Continuous Need*. Nymphomania is unquenchable. While this unquenchability sometimes takes the form of an incapacity to have an orgasm, this seems to be rare. Most nymphomaniacs achieve orgasm—despite statements to the contrary in the popular and technical literature—and they may have several during an evening; but they are still unsatisfied. So, they soon require more sex. And more. Sooner or later, this means that they must resort to different men, and to many men.

The nymphomaniac's unquenchability may not necessarily take the form of additional need the same night. For the moment, the fires may be quenched sufficiently, offering a release from tensions. But the rapidity with which the tensions re-arise, and the lack of control which the woman has over them, indicate the desires are insatiable.

3. *Compulsivity*. Nymphomania is a compulsive form of sexual behavior. By this is meant not only that it is beyond control and leads to irrational and self-defeating activities, but that the woman is driven *to actions which she may seek in vain to stop*. Compulsivity of any type, whether it be in the realm of cleanliness, study, work or sex, is always an indication of emotional ill health. Even when the compulsion leads to achievement, it does so for the wrong reasons, and cannot be truly satisfying. Moreover, most compulsive activities are untrustworthy and often lead to self-destructive acts, because they result in a person having decisions made for her (that is, being driven to act), rather than her making decisions for herself.

4. *Self-Contempt*. Nymphomania has one characteristic that frequently does not accompany other compulsive desires. It is generally looked upon by society—which means by the nymphomaniac as well as by those around her—as degrading. In this respect, nymphomania finds

20

itself in that group of deviant activities which are condemned in our culture, not because they are the most harmful to the community, but because they are the most sexual.

The girl who suffers from compulsive desires to overeat may still have a fairly acceptable image of herself; she may feel a sense of worth, may be able to hold her head high and believe that hers is a worthwhile life. She may wish she were thinner, but she does not wish she were dead. And so it is with many other neurotics or compulsives.

Because her area of compulsive activity is sexual, the nymphomaniac tends to accept the condemnatory judgments of society, of her friends and family, and even of her lovers and pickups. She is filled with self-contempt, looks upon herself as dirty, is often masochistic, and is generally dependent. Unlike those suffering from nonsexual compulsions, she frequently conceals her interests from many of her friends, business associates, and family members.

Thus, the nymphomaniac is anxiety-ridden and disturbed, not only because her hypersexuality is a symptom of deep disturbance, but also because *the symptom itself results in further self-denigration*. Her secondary set of anxieties may become more self-defeating than the difficulties from which her nymphomania originally stemmed.

In this way the nymphomaniac is caught in a vicious (and dynamic) circle. On the one hand, her uncontrollable promiscuity is a symptom of emotional disturbances, and on the other hand it causes new and aggravated disturbances. Thus arises a ceaseless momentum, which cannot help but worsen if therapeutic assistance is not sought.

In *The Art and Science of Love* (Ellis, 1960), as in many other texts, a distinction is made between so-called and true nymphomania. *True* nymphomania, according to this distinction, "exists when a woman has intense desire which is not relieved by intercourse or orgasm and which may drive her to near-madness. In its true form it is exceptionally rare and, like most anomalies of this type, seems to be caused by unusual conditions of neuromuscular disease."

The vast majority of women who are described in the literature as "nymphomaniacs" are nothing but highly-sexed females who are quite promiscuous and whose behavior would hardly be noticed if they were males. True nymphomaniacs are seldom found outside the disturbed wards of mental hospitals.

True or endogenous nymphomania is somewhat akin to priapism (an almost constant erection) in the male, and is a rare disorder. In my many years of clinical practice and sex research, not a single case of this extreme form of female hypersexuality has been encountered.

Frequently found, however, has been *compulsive promiscuity,* usually psychologically caused, in which the woman is capable of having some measure of sex-love satisfaction but nonetheless drives herself, in a self-defeating pattern, from one man to another. When we speak of nymphomania in this book, we shall (unless otherwise indicated) refer to this kind of *compulsive promiscuity,* and not to true or endogenous nymphomania, which is more a physiological than a psychological entity. Of course, we will not use the term nymphomania to describe a highly-sexed, noncompulsive woman who enjoys sex relations with a number of males and who never gets herself into emotional difficulties because of her promiscuous behavior.

2

Nymphomaniacs through the Ages

ALTHOUGH SUSAN WAS BUT FIFTEEN WHEN SHE EM-
barked on her course of indiscriminate sexuality, she had
some illustrious predecessors who were even younger when
they began their promiscuous sex lives. One of these women
became so famous that she lent her name to the medical
syndrome of the oversexed female, known as the Messalina
complex. Her story is found in the most authentic primary
sources of Roman history (Suetonius, 1939), in the best of
the secondary sources (Brittain, 1907; Durant, 1944), as well
as in numerous pieces of historical fiction (Oleck, 1959).

Messalina

Valeria Messalina was sixteen when she married Claudius,
then forty-eight. Her husband had already had three wives
and numerous mistresses, but though Messalina was but one-
third his age, and had probably embarked on a career of
sexuality only two or three years earlier, she may have
already counted as many partners as he could. "She was not
unusually pretty," Durant tell us: "her head was flat, her face
florid, her chest malformed; but a woman need not be beautiful to commit adultery."

It was convenient to be the wife of the Emperor, for
Messalina fell in and out of love with ease, and each time a
man rejected her advances, she appealed to Claudius for
help, and her husband would order his subject to be obedient
to her whims.

Messalina's husband Claudius was, according to Suetonius,
"immoderate in his passion for women," and she not less so
in her desire for men. Another historian, Dio Cassius
(1905), says that it was Messalina who gave Claudius attractive housemaids for bedfellows, while Juvenal reports, perhaps unfairly, that she would disguise herself, enter a brothel,
receive all comers, and pocket the fees.

Another story of a mating between a highly-sexed male and a highly-sexed female in the Roman power structure centers around Tiberius and his wife Julia who is usually described as a nymphomaniac. Julia was first married at the age of fourteen, but her youthful husband died two years later. She mourned, and then enjoyed a freedom that she had already begun to desire. At eighteen, she was again married, this time to a man of forty-two. She is said to have had many affairs during the brief marriage in which she gave her husband five children. He, too, died—after nine years of marriage. Three years later, having filled the empire with gossip, rumors, and scandal, she married Tiberius, but continued her full sex life. Finally, Tiberius retired from public office, and allowed his wife to be a free woman. Of the period that followed, Durant writes: "Julia passed from one lover to another, and the revels of her set filled the Forum with turmoil at night." Another writer (R. E. L. Masters, 1963), whose description of Julia's activities shows her as almost a classic nymphomaniac, says:

Julia was the daughter of the Emperor Augustus, absolute ruler over one hundred million souls. She was beautiful, intelligent, highly educated and witty. A patroness of the arts, she could win and hold on her intellectual merits the friendship of men like the poet Ovid. Everything a woman might want was hers—save for sexual satisfaction; and this not ten men, nor a hundred, nor a thousand could provide.

Scarcely a male lived who could not arouse Julia to a fever pitch of desire. If a boy's organ was capable of erection, he was old enough; and even if he were not, there were other uses for little boys.... As for old men, they too could perform in at least some way; and in between these extremities of unsteady youth and unsteady decrepitude, any man at all would do.

Even as a young girl this daughter of an Emperor had delighted in exhibiting her body publicly, preferring translucent garments designed to reveal all and suggest more. Also as little more than a child, she had embarked upon her amorous adventures, soon numbering her lovers in the scores, and eventually in the hundreds. Long before her marriage to Tiberius, Julia's public drunkenness and sexual excesses were a commonplace of Roman gossip, which delighted in nothing more than the erotic extravagances of the famous....

From the arms of her innumerable lovers, said to

encompass half the handsome youths and virile warriors of Rome, she moved on to the practice of offering herself to every passing stranger, whatever his color, age or appearance. With a band of lascivious Roman women she wandered through the streets, accosting passersby and sometimes dragging them into the nearest alleyway or archway, where the transaction would be swiftly concluded in order that another might be the more quickly begun. . . .

At night she would take up her post by the statue of Marsyas in the Forum, a well-known resort of prostitutes. No man was turned away; no desire, however vicious or grotesque, was permitted to go unfulfilled.

George Sand

In the examination of some of the biographical information about presumably promiscuous women, it becomes clear that many writers have been confused by nymphomania and oversexuality. Some have described as nymphomaniacs older women deeply interested in and involved with young men, while other historians have shown their own prejudices and misapprehensions about things sexual by labeling as nymphomaniacs women who continue their active sex lives when their chronological age has reached the seventies, and higher.

For example, take George Sand the well-known French writer, a prolific novelist who poured out thousands of pages of embellished, thinly disguised autobiography. Her loves were several, and often her lovers were as famous as she herself, thus constituting liaisons that would attract attention during her lifetime and would fascinate biographers for years afterwards. She married early, was divorced soon after, and entered upon a career as a writer that was to bring her into contact (literally as well as figuratively) with many notable contemporaries.

Then there followed a string of lovers, with some affairs beginning before others ended. Nevertheless, George Sand was emotionally involved with just about all these men. There was a youthful lawyer Jules Sandeau, with whom she lived for a year, or perhaps a little longer; it was the discovery of *his* infidelities, not hers, that caused the affair to terminate. At which point she wrote to her friend Sainte-Beuve: "My heart is a cemetery!"—hardly the words of a woman who was discarding her lovers for new ones as quickly as the latter could be obtained.

A little later, perhaps as she approached the age of thirty,

25

she became passionately involved with Alfred de Musset. The period between Sandeau and de Musset was hardly a continent one. But while in the midst of the Musset affair, George Sand met and was taken with a physician named Pagello, and off they went to Paris—where she soon grew tired of her new lover.

In one of her novels, written shortly after the Musset-Pagello triangle, a protagonist states: "I have never imposed constancy on myself. When I have felt that love was dead, I have said so without shame or remorse and have obeyed Providence that was leading me elsewhere."

After Alfred de Musset there came Chopin, preceded perhaps by Liszt, who was surely a close friend and probably her lover. And so it continued, until she died at the age of seventy-two. Passionate and romantic loves, finding sexual expression, were continued into her late years, with interest centered frequently in youthful lovers.

George Sand lived what was popularly known, a generation or two ago, as a life of free love. She was deeply engaged, long before the movement was popular, in the struggle for women's rights, and she saw as part of this struggle the right of a woman to have as unrestricted a sexual life as does a man. Biographers and commentators who speak of her as oversexed or as a nymphomaniac are usually betraying their own devotion to the double standard, their antifeminist concepts, and their misunderstanding of the role of a free woman in a sexually free society. If George Sand's novels are today dated and little read, she nevertheless stands out as a greatly talented woman *whose sex life did not inhibit her from functioning fully in her society*. There is no evidence that, for her, sexual freedom was a result of disturbing factors in her childhood or adolescence, nor that it resulted from problems of compulsivity that today would be called anxiety-producing. That she came in sharp conflict with her society is hardly deniable; that she handled this conflict in a self-satisfying manner, seems equally true. *She had a sex life, not an oversexed life,* and this is what appears to confuse so many of her biographers and historians.

Theodora, Wife of the Emperor Justinian

When we turn to some of the women of *power*, rather than of talent, and if we believe that historical documents reflect reality, we are confronted with oversexuality, if not nymphomania with its compulsive aspect. One good example is Theodora, the wife of Emperor Justinian who reigned from A.D. 527 to 565. He left the body of laws which have so greatly influenced Western civilization, the Justinian codes. These codes, ironically enough, reflect and reinforce many antisexual fears, beliefs, and prejudices.

A historical document, probably authentic, attributed to Procopius, a contemporary of Justinian, was translated and published (Richard Atwater, 1934). According to Atwater, Procopius found himself out of favor with the Emperor; Procopius thereupon wrote a sycophantic report on the architectural achievements of Justinian, and then, in self-disgust and in atonement for his hypocrisy, wrote what was later called *The Secret History*. A curious document, it narrates the story of the sexual lives and intrigues of Justinian and his wife Theodora, and of their various lovers: their jealousies, humiliations, rapes, seductions, and orgies. The author describes Theodora as the "most depraved of all courtesans," a woman who "did not wait to be asked by anyone she met, but on the contrary, with inviting jests and a comic flaunting of her skirts herself tempted all men who passed by, especially those who were adolescent." Thus far, Theodora appears not much different than any flirtatious girl. However:

> On the field of pleasure she was never defeated. Often she would go picnicking with ten young men or more, in the flower of their strength and virility, and dallied with them all, the whole night through. When they wearied of the sport, she would approach their servants, perhaps thirty in number, and fight a duel with each of these, and even thus found no allayment of her craving. Once, visiting the house of an illustrious gentleman, they say she mounted the projecting corner of her dining couch, pulled up the front of her dress, without a blush, and thus carelessly showed her wantoness. And though she flung wide three gates to the ambassadors of Cupid, she lamented that nature had not similarly unlocked the straits of her bosom, that she might there have contrived a further welcome to his emissaries.

(For those not familiar with the symbolism of Procopius, the three gates referred to are the vagina, anus, and mouth.)

Theodora became pregnant frequently, but aborted herself with ease. She unblushingly and unhesitatingly disrobed in public, not quite to the last garment (as she could not disobey the law against nudity), but sufficiently to alarm and arouse the public. She walked onto the stage of a public

27

theatre more than half-naked, covered only with a ribbon. There she would recline on her back:

Slaves to whom the duty was entrusted would then scatter grains of barley from above into the calyx of this passion flower, whence geese, trained for the purpose, would next pick the grains one by one with their bills and eat. When she rose, it was not with a blush, but she seemed to glory in the performance.

Thus were Theodora's exploits, conquests, and exhibitions chronicled. She did not seem restrained, this historian tells us, to undress in the midst of a group of actors, "and arch her back provocatively, advertising like a peacock, both to those who had experience of her and to those who had not yet had that privilege, her trained suppleness."

Whether Procopius has embellished the achievements of his characters to vént his hatred, we leave to historians to determine; for our part, we can affirm that he has given us a portrait of a disturbed woman: a *sexually unquenchable* female whose nymphomania was probably combined with exhibitionistic self-contempt, self-doubt, and self-hatred, which flowered into a despotic will for power.

Other legendary nymphomaniacs are recorded. There is said to have been a Queen Zingua of Angola, who ruled in the early seventeenth century, and who kept a harem of males. Among the Queen's exploits and pastimes were to dress the male lovers in women's clothes, to have pregnant females executed, to spend the night with a lover and then watch his execution in the morning, and to arrange a battle to the death between two athletes, and then hop into bed with the winner. Zingua is said to have continued her active sex life past the age of seventy; then, at the age of seventy-seven, she became a convert to Catholicism.

And finally a word about Catherine the Great, Empress of Russia, a woman of power whose name has frequently been linked with various sexual excesses, heterosexual and homosexual, including voyeurism. The rumors concerning the life of Catherine are so numerous that it is, today, difficult to separate the fact from fiction. She admitted having a dozen lovers, but some biographers assign her several hundred. One report has it that she died in the act of copulation—certainly possible. And it is said that in her old age, not satisfied with her sex life (she is quoted as having advocated sexual relations six times a day), she enjoyed watching sex orgies in which she was not participating. She changed her lovers often, and was mainly interested in their sex organs—not in them as persons.

Catherine explained that she was cursed with insomnia, and that sexuality was merely a means of putting herself to sleep.

Potiphar's Wife

It is when we turn to the portrayal of sex in the Bible, that we find a difference between the interest of a woman in one man to whom she is not wedded, and the interest of a woman in all men—*any* man. This contrast is clear in the story of Joseph and Potiphar's wife.

Potiphar was the captain in the Egyptian army who bought Joseph from the Midianites. One authority (Zenos, 1936) suggests that the office he occupied, in Hebrew, meant eunuch; and inasmuch as the use of eunuchs as military officers was common in many periods of history, it is not unlikely that the story of Potiphar's wife is that of a woman married to a eunuch.

Potiphar is first introduced into the Biblical story when he purchases Joseph:

And the Midianites sold him [Joseph] into Egypt unto Potiphar, an officer of Pharaoh's, the captain of the guard.

Potiphar brought Joseph into his own home: *"And Joseph was of beautiful form, and fair to look upon,"* a situation that might tempt any woman, even if not married to a eunuch. And the wife of this army officer was no exception:

And it came to pass after these things, that his master's wife cast her eyes upon Joseph; and she said: "Lie with me." But he refused, and said unto his master's wife: "Behold, my master, having me, knoweth not what is in the house, and he hath put all that he hath into my hand; he is not greater in this house than I; neither hath he kept back any thing from me but thee, because thou art his wife. How then can I do this great wickedness, and sin against God?"

Here we see that Potiphar's wife was not going to lose any time with subtle hints that might be misunderstood. She wanted Joseph, and she simply told him so. In a fictional study (Mann, 1938) of the efforts of Potiphar's wife (identified as Mut-em-enet) to seduce Joseph, the author deals with the "frightfully direct and frank expression which tradition puts in her mouth: *'lie with me.'* "

So direct, indeed, so frank, that it sounds like a lewd proposal coming from a woman who made it quite naturally and at small cost to herself, instead of being the final outcry of her utter agony of spirit and flesh.

The wife of Potiphar would not leave Joseph alone—day after day she entreated him, and day after day he refused. "He hearkened not unto her, to lie by her, or to bed with her."

Traditionally, the term *Potiphar's wife* has been associated with a sexually *indiscriminate* woman, which she indeed may have been, although there is no evidence of it in the Biblical story. Although commonly referred to as a nymphomaniac, the more reasonable assumption is that she was a sexually interested and awakened *w*oman.

There is little to indicate that the woman was throwing herself at others as shamelessly as she did at Joseph. In fact, quite the contrary. For *if all she wanted was a man,* she would not have beckoned to Joseph day after day, nor have been dismayed by his indifference or refusal.

The story of Potiphar's wife illustrates vividly the difference between nymphomania and *extramarital sexual interest.* This woman was not in need of all men, or of any man, or of just a man, but of a *particular* man. She was fixated on one person, and she had to have him. (If her interests in Joseph were nonsexual as well as sexual, we would then speak of her as being *in love* with him, in the manner that Constance Chatterley was in love with her gardener Mellors.)

Whereas nymphomania is indiscriminate, love is the opposite; it is so completely discriminating that it regards one and only one individual as a proper or desirable sex object. Potiphar's wife wanted her man badly; she was irrational about it; she was willing to risk punishment if she could have him.

Many have pondered over the character of the would-be seductress of Joseph. The answer of Thomas Mann is of great interest:

Was she a nymphomaniac? A loose woman? The idea is

30

absurd. Mut-em-enet was a saint, a chaste moon-nun of high social position, whose strength was consumed partly in the demands of her highly cultured life, but partly, so to speak, was temple property and transmuted into spiritual pride.

Interestingly enough, the wife of Potiphar is never punished.

Much of the misunderstanding and mythology of nymphomania derives from its confusion with adultery, prostitution, discriminating and controlled promiscuity, and even with the strict monogamy of the sexually-awakened woman whose interests are confined to her marriage bed.

It is the *rejection* of Potiphar's wife by Joseph that presents some interesting problems related to modern women, and which suggests one more delineation of nymphomania. Most women interested in sexual relations with a specific man do not have to resort to dramatic supplications. They know that they need offer but slight encouragement—if the man is interested, he will take it from there. Unlike Joseph, he will respond to her advances, and may well end up thinking he has been the aggressor—and she may come to the same wishful conclusion. The manner in which this process works has been described in *Sex and the Single Girl* (Brown, 1962), and detailed instructions as to how the girl can manipulate the man she wants until she gets him are given in *The Intelligent Woman's Guide to Man-Hunting* (Ellis, 1963b). But what if the girl's selected lover does stand steadfast and continues to say *no?* Any rational girl would consider the young man mentally ill, and would move on.

It was the feeling of rejection, after she had thrown herself at him, that disturbed Potiphar's wife. And some modern girls would be deeply upset by this, too. Instead of asking: "What's wrong with him?" they would think: "What's wrong with me?"

The *nymphomaniac*, however, although unhappy about being rejected, is rarely that much involved with one man. Her involvement is with *men*—she cannot be concerned with a single rejection. She feels there are many more men where this new sex partner came from, and most of them can be had with ease.

When we turn our attention from Potiphar's wife to Messalina and to Catherine, an entirely different story unfolds, for here sexuality is utilized as part of the power struggle. First, since it is always considered degenerate to be as dramatically

31

highly sexed as these women, their enemies use exaggeration and gossip to get them off the throne—or to keep them from being the power behind it. Second, sex is usually not a goal in itself for these women, it is part of their megalomaniacal need: their urge to lord over, to utilize, and to destroy (rather than to love) men.

In royalty as in plebian life, nymphomania is anxiety-producing, disruptive, and disturbing. It is also no longer an individual affair; it becomes a public problem.

3

The Myth of Nymphomania

THAT TRUE PHYSIOLOGICAL NYMPHOMANIA SEEMS TO be a relatively rare phenomenon has been generally accepted. But during the past decade, there has been a growing understanding that widespread promiscuity among American females exists from coast to coast. Suburbia, in particular, is singled out as one vast bed of sin. The easiest conclusion, and certainly a frequent one, is: "There must be an awful lot of nymphomaniacs around."

A lack of scientific data, plus the emotional charge that all sexual matters hold in our society, reinforces the popular misunderstanding of nymphomania. If a movie actress changes legal and less-than-legal mates, millions of men and women (consciously and unconsciously wishing they could emulate her activities) gasp—and formulate the idea that all actresses are sex-driven; with the cheerful abandon that characterizes a mob, the popular diagnosis given this behavior is *nymphomania.*

Or ... shocked parents and others in the respectable community learn of a previously proper group of teenage boys and girls who have been having orgiastic sex parties. And an image of "typical" teenage middle-class suburbia is imprinted on the public mind. "These girls must be nymphomaniacs."

As the adult male denounces these degenerates, he wonders why, with so many of them around, *he* can't find one. Maybe it is because these girls are *not* as common as sensational stories would lead us to believe.

On the other hand, some genuinely sex-driven girls are not as likely to come to the attention of the public as would other emotionally disturbed people, including those involved in different types of non-normative sexual behavior. A compulsive girl, in extreme need of frequent and variegated sexual encounters, can find them with ease. Often she can locate partners among men who are not aware that she is the aggressor. They believe they have made a conquest, and are sometimes surprised to learn that the supposedly hard-to-get girl ... isn't. Even if she seduces the delivery boy, she is not likely to be reported to the police (as *would* be the case if a man were compulsively approaching every young female who came to the door).

Consequently, the general public tends both to over-estimate *and* to underestimate the extent of difficult-to-handle sex drives in women. They overestimate because they overgeneralize from a few instances, and they underestimate because the aberration (if it be such) is so easy to conceal.

When one looks at the statistical studies made by Kinsey and his associates, it is clear that a nondiscriminating sex drive that seeks outlets with any member of the other sex is common among males, uncommon among females. The Kinsey research team reported on 1220 married women who had had premarital intercourse. Of these, 2 per cent had had intercourse with more than 20 partners; an additional 4 per cent had copulated with more than 10 and up to 20 men. When these figures were broken down by the decade of birth, they showed that sexual varietism was higher for those born in the first decade of the twentieth century, than for those born earlier. Varietism, however, decreased slightly for women born between 1910 and 1919, reversing the direction, and making it difficult to describe female promiscuity as a significant social trend. The number of premarital partners also increased according to the age at the time of marriage. Girls who married by the time they were twenty had fewer premarital partners than those who married for the first time after thirty.

These statistics would seem to indicate that extreme promiscuity is rare, for even a total of 25 different sex partners previous to marriage is by no means an indication of *uncontrolled* sex drive. However, the Kinsey researchers point out that the sample "does not adequately represent the lower educational levels, and we do not have sufficient information to predict whether the data from those groups would show a greater or lesser promiscuity. Neither does the sample include histories of females who had done time in penal institutions, and our calculations show that that group is much more promiscuous in its premarital activity."

Most other studies that have been made (Davis, 1929; Hamilton, 1929; Bromley and Britten, 1938), only differentiated between women who have restricted their sex activities to one partner and those who have had more than one. But only seldom is mention made of women who have had very

34

large numbers of lovers (perhaps 100 or more in a year), or who have frequently had sexual relations with casually encountered males, or who were uncontrolled in their search for partners.

When the woman in our society is compared with the man, she is less promiscuous not only in her premarital and extramarital coitus, but in petting as well. The Kinsey group noted that, of 2415 females who had indulged in heterosexual petting before marriage, about 1 per cent indicated that they had had this experience with more than 100 partners. The corresponding figure for males was 8 per cent. Four per cent of the females and 8 per cent of the males reported that they had petted with 51 to 100 members of the other sex. Altogether, 19 per cent of the females, and 37 per cent of the males, petted with 20 or more partners—but only one-half of one per cent of these females and only 10 per cent of these males actually had coitus with over 20 members of the other sex.

These figures suggest a major difference between promiscuity and nymphomania. For approximately five hundred girls reported that they had petted with 20 or more males before their marriage, but only a dozen of these girls admitted intercourse with 20 or more men. What happened to more than 475 others in the sample? Some of them had not had intercourse until after marriage (in fact, half the girls who petted before marriage were virgins on their wedding nights). Others petted with many men but copulated with only a few, discriminating between those who were acceptable for one type of sex activity and those who were acceptable for any type. In other words, these girls were almost invariably *controlled.* They were capable of exercising *discrimination.* By conventional standards, they were promiscuous, but few of them—perhaps none at all from this large sample—could be considered so uncontrolled as to be nymphomaniacs.

What about the married woman who does not confine her activities to her husband? Again, citing the Kinsey studies, most married women do confine their sex activities to their marriages; and in most of the age groups the number of married women engaged in extramarital relations never exceeded about 17 per cent. Of these, only 3 per cent, or a total of less than one-half of one per cent of all the married women in the study, had more than 20 partners in their extramarital careers. It is clear that any *sexually uncontrolled* woman who did get married would appear in this group. But a wife's having even twenty extramarital partners over a period of years would not necessarily mean that she

35

was *compulsive*. She might still have good control and might exercise discrimination.

Selective Promiscuity—What Nymphomania Is Not

It would seem, from the Kinsey figures, that neither true nor emotionally based nymphomania is encountered frequently; what we do often find is the behavior that has recently been described as *selective promiscuity*. "In their essential features," writes one observer (Kirkendall, 1961), "the sex drives of men and women are very much alike. Such points of difference as do exist are due to environmental and psychological factors rather than to innate, biological, characteristics." This would indicate that the level (or energy) of the sex drive in men and in women may be equatable. However, another writer (Shuttleworth, 1959) points to the ease with which males are aroused by stimuli that would be inadequate to incite women. This ease of arousal together with, or as a function of, the different social attitudes toward men and toward women who indulge in intercourse without marriage, can account for the difference in the numbers of partners of men and of women.

Another study, (Benjamin, 1961) leans to the view that "two or three per cent (of women) are far more interested in sex stimuli and sex relations than any man." This figure seems extremely high, and it would indicate either that hypersexuality in women is more common than anyone has supposed, or that among these millions of hypersexed women, there are only a few (the nymphomaniacs) who are unable to control this drive. Perhaps, although "far more interested," most of these women may be willing and able to satisfy their strong interest with one or a few mates.

An example of this difference between selective promiscuity and nymphomania is brought out when we contrast the story as told in *The Frog Pond* (1961) with that told in *The Housewife's Handbook of Selective Promiscuity* by Rey Anthony (1962), both purporting to be autobiographical accounts of what would be described as highly sexed women. The theme of *The Frog Pond* is told in an advertising blurb: "Tormented! Something she couldn't control drove [her] to seek out men who revolted her—big, powerful, crude, hairy, cruel men. [She] needed love but she couldn't take it. She was frozen. She had to be utterly dominated—beaten, whipped, raped!"

Thus, there unfolds a story of self-punishing nymphomania

36

by a guilt-ridden woman who was seeking men who would punish her *because she was punishing herself for seeking men.* "What is this *Thing* that has me in its iron grip, forcing me to go to its way—not only against my own desire at the moment of the crisis—but against all that I hold dear or even pleasant in this life?"

The author is engaged in a struggle *against* her own sex interests and sex drives: she cannot control them, because they control her. They lead her to men she loathes, to acts she despises, and to hatred of herself for being sexually driven. She prays for help, for "mercy enough to let me out of this—not because of what I have done and will do again, *but because I am compelled against my will to do it.*" [Emphasis in original.] *Compulsivity,* then, is the main theme in the sexual misadventures of this narrator.

Rey Anthony began to develop her sex interests at a rather early age. She went through several marriages and, apparently, thirty or forty lovers. At times, she was deeply involved with the man; at other times, she knew him casually, cared but little for him, was out to make her conquest, and then to leave him to himself. Occasionally one man was enough, sometimes several were needed:

"Rey," Bill said, "you're monogamous, and just won't admit it."

"I'm not, I'm not," I remonstrated.

"Oh yes you are," he said. "Look at the way you feel about me. Why don't you go out with some other man?"

"I just haven't seen any man I wanted to go out with. I go with one, and go to bed with him, if I want to."

And again, in a conversation with another man:

"Thorny, I don't know when it will be, but this much I will tell you. I will have sex. I will be in bed with a man. That much you can know. I have played at this 'respectability' as long as I care to. I will now arrange to have sex as a part of my life."

"You just want to be promiscuous."

"If that's being promiscuous, then that's what I want to be."

Between the two books, there are two great differences: for the troubled heroine of *The Frog Pond* there is compulsivity, as against the freedom of choice of the selectively promiscuous Rey Anthony; and *The Frog Pond* heroine en-

37

gages in self-flagellation, as against the self-acceptance experienced by Rey. One woman hates herself for what she is, and the other cannot dream of a life where she would wish to be different.

How frequent, then, is nymphomania? It would depend on how strictly we adhere to our definitions, and how much we link nymphomania with the self-rejection and self-hate which usually characterize it. If we think in terms of *uncontrollability* of sex behavior, and if we view nymphomaniacs as women driven into situations, then it is doubtful if we are talking about even a small percentage of those females who are listed in the Kinsey volumes as having the highest number of male partners. Compulsivity of this type, resulting in sex acts which the indulging female despises, would probably not be characteristic of more than a very small number of women.

The Self-Diagnosed "Nymphomaniac"

If, however, we speak of the self-hating woman who denigrates herself because she has been having frequent extramarital sexual intercourse, *that* percentage is much higher. Many of these women may have one or two extramarital or premarital relationships. They are not compulsively promiscuous; even if they have a dozen lovers, they choose them selectively and have relationships that are rationally controlled. But many of these women define themselves as worthless; they *think of themselves* as nymphomaniacs. Their problem is not lack of control, nor even unusual promiscuity. It is their negative-perfectionistic definition of themselves.

If we count highly promiscuous women, those whose promiscuity is selective and well controlled, and if we include women who, like Rey Anthony, accept themselves fully, we will then be talking about a group of women that is of small but significant size. These females are not *over*sexed; they are *highly* sexed. This may be the group to which Benjamin referred when he opined that they constituted 2 or 3 per cent of the female population.

Thus, the incidence of *nymphomania* is rare—defined with rigorous adherence to the concepts of (*a*) sexual compulsivity, and (*b*) accompanying self-hatred.

38

PART TWO

Patterns

4

The Structure of Nymphomania

MARJORIE L.

MARJORIE WAS A TRUE COMPULSIVE. SHE PERFORMED obsessive-compulsive rituals while eating, washing, cleaning house, and working. Her food habits were particularly unusual: she would insist on going through a list of 20 or 25 vegetables before she'd return to the first. If the first were carrots, for example, and she ate 22 different vegetables with her meals, she wouldn't eat carrots again until she'd gone through the other 21 vegetables.

Marjorie undeviatingly followed these food rituals; and she did the same thing in her sex relations. She would start, for example, with an Italian boy (she herself being of Italian descent), and then could not consider another Italian bedmate for a while. It would have to be a Greek, an Armenian, a Jew, or a member of another group. She'd go through a good many different males, and then allow herself another Italian.

I hypothesized early in our therapeutic relationship that she was deliberately doing this to punish herself, to atone for her sins *in advance*. This is a fairly common custom among many individuals and is in the philosophy and folklore of many peoples. It has been stated in English perhaps best of all by Emerson in his essay on compensation, where he held that just as there is great good in the world, there is compensating evil. If, therefore, you wish to lead a well-rounded life you presumably have to experience as much evil as good. You can't just have a fortunate existence, you must go through some horrors to compensate for your joys.

Marjorie seemed to believe that if she enjoyed herself sexually, punishment would ensue. Consequently, she set up hurdles, and thereby experienced "pain" along with her pleasure. If she followed enough rituals, and atoned *in advance* for the "sin," then presumably the feared punishment would not occur.

I could see that Marjorie created one compulsion after another—with food or sex or cleaning. She admitted this behavior was irrational, and that there was no reason why she should do it. Yet, she said, she felt uncomfortable if she did *not* do it. Invariably, Marjorie gave in to her compulsion. We will learn more about Marjorie in a later chapter.

Many kinds of irrational ideas lead to *compulsive* behavior. There is a general form of obsessive-compulsiveness which leads to more specific modes of rigidity; in the area of sex these modes may take the form of nymphomania or other closely related, equally uncontrollable, drives.

For example, an individual may repeatedly wash her hands because she feels guilty about some act. She believes she can "wash away" the deed. Thus, her guilt leads to compulsiveness. But another person may continually wash her hands because she is anxious about *everything,* and has innumerable symptoms, of which the washing of her hands is but one example.

The same thing may happen in nymphomania. A woman may become a nymphomaniac—a compulsive female who promiscuously indulges in sex—not because she enjoys sex, but because she is driven by fears. For example, she may fear, as in the case of Ruth (which will be related later), that she is too conforming to her parents' ideal and is giving up her own independence; she may compulsively rebel against them. Another woman may fear that she is worthless and unlovable, that she will fail in her relations with men, and that the only way she can hold males is by going to bed with them.

The "nymphomaniacs" discussed in this book are not necessarily obsessive-compulsives, as was Marjorie; but there are such women, and they tend to ritualistic and other self-compelled behavior, which is self-destructive. Most of these obsessive-compulsives are not merely neurotic—they are at least borderline psychotic. These women are usually

40

driven by a demand for *certainty*. They feel they cannot exist in a world where things are uncertain. Therefore, they try to restructure the world, to put it in perfect order.

Characteristically each does this in a number of ways, rather than in a single way. Not only will she repeatedly wash her hands, or engage in promiscuous activities, but she may place all the books in her bookcases in rigid order, and then completely—and equally precisely—reorder them the next day. A good number of these women belong to orthodox religious groups that encourage this behavior. In these groups they are praised for engaging in their self-demanded rituals. Many consider themselves nonreligious and, in the usual sense of the word, they are. But they are religiously devoted to their over-orderly behavior.

One of the usual concomitants of compulsivity is *obsessive ruminativeness*. That is to say, compulsive individuals frequently are obsessed with thoughts, especially negative thoughts such as: they are worthless, they don't deserve to live. Or they can have almost any other kind of ruminative idea—such as a preoccupation with a dress they have just bought, or with the man they love. They just can't get these thoughts out of their heads—or at least they think they can't. These individuals search for things to become obsessed about—and they find them! Although not all obsessive-compulsives are nymphomaniacs, *nymphomaniacs are, with a fair degree of frequency, in the obsessive-compulsive class.*

5

The Conquering Woman

IN A GENERALLY HOSTILE SOCIAL ATMOSPHERE, IN WHICH she is expected to be inferior, overpowered, and conquered, some women feel themselves driven to assert their superiority by being the conquerer. In a world in which Don Juan has been glamorized and idolized, these women have become the feminine counterpart, a Donna Juanita.

Don Juanism is a well-known syndrome in males; it describes the man who constantly chases after new loves, and who conquers one female after another. According to certain Freudian theories, the male Don Juan is really a latent homosexual who wishes to prove himself and to the world that he is not homosexual—so he conquers females. However, we feel that while it may well be that there are a few latent homosexuals among the Don Juans who use this activity to reinforce their own sagging vision of themselves as males, there is every reason to believe that *the majority of Don Juans are heterosexual*, and have, if anything, fewer underlying homosexual motives than have other men.

For the conquering male, there is a novelty about each sex partner. He finds a new stimulus more exciting than an accustomed one. Consequently Don Juanism in the male is frequently the result of this urge for *variety*.

At the same time, some male Don Juans continually go after new females for nonsexual (or so-called ego) reasons. Actually they tend to have low ego-strength, and need to prove how great they are, so they make, or attempt, one conquest after another. They may do this in nonsexual areas; for example, sports. But in sexual fields it is relatively easy to show oneself and others how great one is. Thus, a great deal of Don Juanism is really a *conquest* drive; this is shown by the fact that as soon as the Don Juan male does conquer the female and enjoys her sexually, he loses practically all interest and goes on to a new girl—who may be difficult to get to bed, and who therefore is conceived of as an even more desirable.

Just as the male is often a Don Juan for ego reasons, so is the female highly promiscuous for the same reasons. That is to say, she is not interested in sexual intercourse for its own sake, though she may enjoy this, but she's very much interested in *conquering the male,* getting him to desire her, and perhaps to enjoy her sexually.

It is the conquest itself—not what can be gained from it—which is challenging and exciting. Some highly promiscuous women, after they make the conquest, have a definite *love* need. But there are others who, once they make the conquest and have just a single satisfactory encounter with a male, have no interest in seeing him again—because they must go on to the new one. Dolores, whom I treated for a few years, was of this sort.

DOLORES

Dolores was a twenty-seven-year-old widow. Although her body was attractive, her face was plain—and disfigured.

Dolores was most conscious of her limitations. The scar on her face, the result of an accident at the age of seven or eight, had caused her much childhood anguish. Then, at the age of twelve or thirteen, she began to develop sexually—and soon found herself with an extremely feminine body to go with her disfigured face. She began to take advantage of that fact to accumulate *many* boy-friends. Thus she set out on the road of making conquests, one following upon another.

In her late high school years, Dolores graduated from heavy petting to sexual intercourse. This she enjoyed, but not more than her previous activity. She knew the boys considered intercourse with a girl something special; consequently, she came to believe that true conquest consisted of getting a male into bed. She developed this attitude after she found some of the inexperienced boys over-anxious, frightened, and hence impotent or semi-impotent. They preferred to neck rather than take a chance they might prove inadequate in active copulation. If, then, Dolores could succeed in having her male companion—often a virgin until that night—obtain a full erection, and copulate effectively, that was a successful

43

conquest. Anything else was much less of an achievement to her, hardly worthy of being classified as a conquest.

Before a school term ended, Dolores had dated practically every boy in the class. Later, when she worked in an office, she managed to date—at least once—every man working with her, the married as well as the unmarried, the youthful office boy and the elderly clerk ready for retirement. In many of these instances she would have sex relations.

Once she had "conquered" the male, Dolores was ready to discard him, although he might accept and approve of her. Quite a few partners developed intense affection for her, not only because she was sexually satisfying, but because she was an intelligent person and a good conversationalist. But Dolores had no particular interest in this kind of success. She simply wanted to make the sex conquest, and go on to the next bedmate.

This is not to say Dolores never became enamored of the males. But her affections, when aroused, would be directed toward an *inaccessible* person—perhaps an older man, married, and in an inextricable family position. She would either not see him and would conceal her feelings, or she would see him on a friendly basis without allowing any sexual involvement to develop.

Dolores was able to admit, after the first few sessions of therapy, that she was afraid of allowing affairs to develop with the men she loved, *for fear that she would finally lose them*. So, from time to time she allowed herself to become involved, and remained so for a matter of months, or even years—but these were fantasy loves. They were not reciprocated; there was no attempt to actualize them, and she would just go on thinking about these men—while actually going to bed with other men in whom she had no love interest.

With the men with whom she had her promiscuous, compulsive sex relations, there was a fairly consistent pattern. She would meet them at a dance, or allow herself to be picked up at a beach, park, or on a bus. Then she would go off with the man and start petting. But she would stop him after a while and tell him this was not her interest, she didn't "go in for preliminaries." She wanted the whole thing or nothing.

Dolores would leave it to her partner to find a place, since most of the time she was living with her parents, ostensibly leading a conventional existence. Most males obliged, either by renting a room at a hotel or motel, or making a hasty telephone call to a bachelor friend. Then, with no preliminaries, they proceeded to bed.

When they had had intercourse and her partner had proved himself, he would usually ask to see her again. But Dolores' interest had flagged. She became vague and indefinite. She managed not to be available again, and would go on to the next man, and the next, following much the same pattern.

Often, to the surprise of her partner, Dolores was able to induce a man to have multiple orgasms. Because of her technique and encouragement, he surpassed his own expectations, and this he communicated to her in many ways. All of which pleased Dolores, as it proved to her that she was highly desirable.

There are many women in our society who must prove themselves by conquest after conquest. We shall return to Dolores to show how her pattern could be (and was) modified. Let us look at a similar pattern in Isabel.

ISABEL

An attractive girl, Isabel could not possibly have developed a sense of inadequacy because of her appearance. She was a girl of only average intelligence, raised in a family that worshipped intellectual ability, and Isabel had severe feelings of doubt about herself in many areas. Consequently, she went from one sexual conquest to another, to divert self-confrontation with her supposed inadequacies. Because she was so successful at sex (she, too, developed a sexual adeptness far above the average), Isabel could relax and forget, at least momentarily, her real and her imagined inadequacies in other respects.

Isabel's sickness was one of frantic diversion. She worked a few weeks, then decided to marry. She became pregnant and, thus, could stay home. Isabel took care of her child for a while, but then managed to become sick. Unable to continue caring for the baby, she was given nursing help.

Whenever a situation demanded any degree of competence, Isabel would scoot away in panic. The one exception was her sexual conquests.

Having proved her competence, Isabel refused to stop these activities even after marriage. Some affairs were discreet, while others were so open they were even known to Isabel's husband, who gave his tacit assent because he was afraid to lose her.

Isabel would go to bed with a man once, prove to be perfectly satisfactory to him and to herself, since she enjoyed

45

the sex relations, and then rush on to the next fellow. She never became deeply involved with any male (including her husband, whose acceptance of her she just tolerated), because she feared the more involved she became, the more the man would discover about her nonsexual incompetence.

To Isabel, marriage, like life generally, was an evasion of responsibilities. She chose a husband who would accept her deficiencies because he was impressed by her looks and sexual ability.

Isabel, as did Dolores, went for *conquest*. She had nothing else in life, made no attempt whatsoever to build toward nonsexual rewards, and seemed to be happy only at the height of these conquests.

Dolores would be considered a severely neurotic girl; Isabel tended more to the borderline psychotic area because she had *almost total inadequacy feelings*. She just couldn't see herself succeeding in life. She gave up, early in the game, and made no attempt to do what she really wanted to do.

Like Isabel, many nymphomaniacs fall into one affair after another because it *distracts* them from the effects of their general disorganization—and they win male acceptance at the same time. Sometimes they are sexually or amatively successful in their affairs; but even if they aren't, *at least something is going on*. These women tend to lead dull lives aside from these affairs. The series of sexual relationships gives them *something* to live for. At least they know that after one affair has ended there will be another, and then another.

Some promiscuous females believe there is a magic solution to their problems—that if they have a long series of affairs, at some point Prince Charming will come along and their life will be completely changed (without, of course, their making any effort to change it). However, Isabel didn't believe this. She considered herself, as do many borderline psychotics, absolutely hopeless, waiting for the day she would finally die.

Often, in a depressed mood, she contemplated suicide.

Though Isabel recognized, after a while, that none of her affairs was final, and that none would lead anywhere, she still found them interesting and absorbing diversions. Her Donna Juanitaism was a function of a borderline psychotic state, a "solution" to the problem she felt had no solution whatsoever.

Donna Juanita is a not uncommon pattern for the compulsively promiscuous female to follow; it is a particularly self-defeating one, even more self-defeating than is the male Don Juan pattern. It leaves in the wake of the conquering woman only a history of frustration for herself, her conquered males and her husband. Fortunately, it is a problem which, as we shall discuss, is usually amenable to modification through guidance, counseling, and psychotherapy.

6

Prostitution and Nymphomania

THE WORD *nymphomania* AND, PARTICULARLY, ITS diminutive, *nympho,* are often used too freely, without regard for their actual meanings. They do not refer to anyone of an evil character, but only to a woman for whom contempt is expressed because she is relatively highly sexed and is not reluctant to have frequent sexual encounters. One other term is loosely used in the same manner, namely *whore;* in the minds of many people, the two terms are interchangeable. These people believe nymphomaniacs are, or will become whores, and "no one would be a whore unless she were a nympho." Paradoxically, there is also widespread belief that prostitutes are frigid.

Some of the most interesting definitions of prostitution are summarized in a recent study (Henriques, 1963): Starting with the Oxford English Dictionary, Henriques quotes the definition: "The offering of the body to indiscriminate lewdness for hire." A little later, he provides a legal definition: "Prostitution means the offering for reward by a female of her body commonly for purposes of general lewdness. It is not necessary to prove that the offer was for the purpose of natural sexual connection." And, from the United States, a "legal pronouncement that a common prostitute is a woman who submits herself to indiscriminate sexual intercourse with or without hire."

But when one British commentator refers to the prostitute as "a woman or girl who for purposes of financial gain, without emotional sanction or selection, supplies the male demand for physiological sex gratification," Henriques comments that this "leaves out of consideration the case of the nymphomaniac who deliberately chooses to prostitute herself through her craving for varied sexual intercourse."

The suggestion that prostitution "is distinguished by the

elements of hire, promiscuity, and emotional indifference" (Davis, 1937) might, in fact, eliminate the emotionally involved nymphomaniac who indulges in prostitutive acts. Another writer. (Benjamin, 1961) comments that the usual "and rather narrow definition of prostitution is 'promiscuous intercourse for hire,' to which, however, can and should be added that such intercourse is largely indiscriminate, without affection, and frequently anonymous, payment being made in cash."

The word prostitution has, in fact, been used at times to categorize any sexual intercourse for nonsexual gain. This would make a prostitute of a woman who has but one lover, if the motivation in her sex life with him is to obtain money—or even companionship. Such a definition includes the frigid wife who unwillingly indulges in what, to her, is a distasteful act to keep the marriage together. Obviously, such a definition is inadequate, for it fails to differentiate among essentially different situations.

The term prostitute is also misused to categorize any girl having non-marital sex relations for sexual and affectional gratification, even when such relations are limited to one partner with whom there is serious involvement. Here, the word is used as a synonym for immoral, which in turn is applied indiscriminately to the sexually awakened female.

At another extreme, the concept of prostitution has been applied to all those (particularly women) who engage in promiscuous, indiscriminate sexual affairs. It is this definition that equates the prostitute and the nymphomaniac in popular opinion.

Today, the best definition of the prostitute is probably a paraphrase of Benjamin's: Prostitution is the indiscriminate indulgence of an individual in sexual relationships with many persons, for monetary reward. While this definition would include the male prostitute, the young man who finds an older woman to give him money, and the female who grants sexual favors to other females in return for money—we are here concerned with none of these categories. The prostitute with whom we are concerned is the woman granting sexual rights or favors to many men, almost without discrimination, and for a fee. She may be an expensive call girl, or a party girl used by businessmen; she may be a regular worker at a brothel (a disappearing establishment in American life); she may be a bar-hopper, street-walker, or a well-dressed young lady who frequents fashionable hotel lobbies. Whatever her method of finding clients, she is relatively non-selective, will have sexual intercourse with people she has previously never seen, and *always* expects payment.

It would seem, upon first observation, that the compulsively hypersexed woman would naturally gravitate toward prostitution as a profession. "Why give it away for nothing?" her friends will ask her, or she will ask herself. "If I have to have a man so often, and will take any guy who comes along, why not make it pay?"

Nevertheless, an examination of the studies made of prostitutes reveals that *few of them are highly sexed or have drives in any way resembling nymphomania.* The literature abounds with instances and statements (some of which may be exaggerated) that indicate the opposite. According to authorities who have interviewed large numbers of prostitutes, far from being oversexed, many fit the following groups:

1. Frigid women, who actually despise sex and the man with whom they are copulating, and who (according to Freudian interpretation) use the sex act to take money from the man because of this revulsion.

2. Lesbians, who find their affectional and erotic release in the arms of other women, often themselves prostitutes or, recently, female pimps (Corey, 1964; Benjamin and Masters, 1964).

It can be seen that these two categories are not necessarily mutually exclusive. Frigid women and lesbians may lust after men; but, because of antisexual upbringing, or antimale prejudices, they may embody their lust in a matrix of hatred and resentment. Consequently, they may gratify their unconscious craving—and conscious loathing—by pretending to themselves that their sole copulatory purpose is monetary gain.

Benjamin cites eight advantages that women derive from prostitution, including money, romance, adventure, and satisfaction of neurotic needs; he points to the gratification of strong sex drives (that might correspond, to some extent, to nymphomania) as one of these advantages:

A small minority of prostitutes are so highly sexed that they actually enjoy many or most of their sex participations, and these women find a life of prostitution virtually ideal. Kinsey and his associates find that although many women are not as easily aroused or as highly sexed as are men, 2 or 3 per cent are far more interested in sex stimuli and sex relations than any man. It is likely that some prostitutes are in this group.

Another writer, in his description of status-seeking, pyramid-climbing call girls and party girls (Greenwald, 1958), did not find in them high sex drives or insatiable sex cravings. Nymphomaniacs would probably not adjust well to the life of the call girl he describes. Researchers who have studied prostitution to determine why women take to this trade, have come up with many reasons. A combination of causes seems to be present in most cases; among those cited most frequently are: economic need, cultural conditioning, emotional disturbances (particularly, masochistic trends), rebellion against societal values, desire to obtain ease and comfort without difficulty, definition of themselves in non-prostitutional terms, and, finally, sexual drive and interest in men, leading to utilization of this interest for monetary gain.

It is this last category that alone would be pertinent to the study of nymphomania. However, as an explanation for prostitution in general, it is of relatively little value since it applies to the few cases where the drive and interest *usually* are normal and controllable, rather than compulsive. Usually—but not always. Cases of girls entering prostitution as a career to combine their out-of-control interest in males with financial gain, are not unknown.

The Emotionally Motivated Semi-Professional

Many compulsive hypersexed women become *semi*-professionals—especially when they reside in large cities. They are seen in certain areas, alone or with another girl, always on the lookout, ready to strike up a conversation with an attractive man. They make it clear that they are not prostitutes —but that they *can* use a five- or ten-dollar bill. Unlike prostitutes, they can be talked into participating in sex without pay—although there is almost always a drink to be purchased, sometimes a meal. To these women the sex act is not a financial transaction.

One girl in this group, when interviewed, displayed a tremendous antagonism toward "whores." "She's nothing but a whore, she'll go with any guy who'll give her five bucks," she said of an acquaintance. "She's a slut," she commented about another.

"What's a slut?"
"A whore," the girl replied.

51

"You'll take money, won't you?"

"If the guy has it, and wants to give it."

"Then how are you different from her?"

"I like the guy, and I'll go with him anyway. Sure, I got to eat. But I won't do it just for the money. And not with *anybody*."

Nevertheless, in the United States there are a number of highly-sexed, *self-defined nymphomaniacs* who drift into full-time prostitution. What happens to them once they become prostitutes? Following are typical developments:

1. There tends to be considerable antagonism between the few highly-sexed, largely compulsive, heterosexually awakened, and heterosexually oriented prostitutes, and the run-of-the-mill prostitutes who look upon this as just another way of life and obtain little or no pleasure out of their lucrative sexual acts. The term "nympho" is often heard among prostitutes as a term of contempt; one is not supposed to go with men because of a strong desire, although this is permissible with one particular lover. Nevertheless, for prostitutes to have sexual intercourse *only* for the money that comes with it is unusual. This is often a pretense. In reality, the prostitute, deprived of her paying men, usually turns to other forms of sex outlet (as is seen in prison).

Nymphomaniacs, in turn, feel contempt for ordinary prostitutes. This contempt may often be defensive—as the armor of those who have been reviled, and who spew forth the same hate that was heaped upon them.

2. The *nymphomaniac* finds it extremely difficult to become a successful prostitute. First, because she sometimes becomes deeply involved with a customer, which he often discovers and uses as grounds to gain repeated sex favors without pay. Second, because she is so often willing to give herself gratis. Third, because she now finds it difficult to be as discriminating as she was before turning professional.

3. The *nymphomaniac* prostitute is resented by other prostitutes, who discover that she has cheated, has violated the rules by giving men more than their money's worth, and not receiving commensurate remuneration.

4. The large number of customers a prostitute has to take on unselectively (as in a brothel or at a convention) is particularly disturbing to the *nymphomaniac*, who usually

makes one of these two adjustments: *(a)* she abandons indiscriminate prostitution in favor of selective promiscuity, continuing to obtain fees when she can, but primarily seeking the *partner,* not the fee; or *(b)* she adjusts herself to the normative order of the average prostitute, losing interest in the sex act as an act of stimulation, regarding it as a means to an economic end. In a sense, *she may be cured of her nymphomania*—by using it as a transitional bridge into prostitution!

Nevertheless, prostitutes and nymphomaniacs have an element in common: their extremely frequent sexual encounters with different males in a manner that society condemns. Most prostitutes, and nymphomaniacs to some extent, internalize this condemnation, feel self-contempt and shame. And each group, peculiarly enough, tries to clearly differentiate itself from the other in an attempt to be protected from indiscriminate social opprobrium.

7

Neurotic Mating

GAIL

SEVERAL HOMOSEXUAL-NYMPHOMANIAC MATINGS HAVE come to our attention during recent years. There was Gail, a thirty-year-old woman who did not come for psychotherapy because of her sex problems. She had ulcers and was recommended for psychotherapy by her physician. Gail had been married, and she had a son of seven. At the time I saw her, she had been married for a year to a thirty-five-year-old homosexual, Burt. He was attached to her child and had always wanted to be a father and a family man. She felt that he was reasonably fond of her, although their marriage was without sex. His interests were known to her before they were married, but she looked upon Burt as "a nice guy," and appreciated that together they could make a home for the child and for each other.

Burt had a long history of casual sex relations with males, but without serious attachments. Gail was his main object of affection, though not of erotic interest.

On the other hand, Gail had had several long-term affairs with males, including her previous marriage which had lasted about four years. She preferred to have a steady sex-love relationship, but had not been able to achieve one in recent years. Embittered and despondent, she had begun promiscuous relations on a highly compulsive basis.

Gail fell into the category of nymphomaniacs who are driven to their compulsive promiscuity by their *need to be loved*. She really wanted to win male approval, but was never able to do so on a nonsexual basis. Somewhat plain in appearance, although not as unattractive as she thought, Gail had a low sense of adequacy coupled with a high level of aspiration. She went for men who were good looking—and who were also intelligent and cultured. She was just not in their class, and they tended to leave her shortly after the relationship had started. These men were mainly interested in sex, nothing else; and she compulsively continued her search for relations with them because she could not bear to be alone and unloved. She thought that one of these days she would really win one of them.

Now, Gail had found security. Burt was the intelligent and cultured man she sought, and he would never desert her. Both of them lived with a mask, pretending to the world that theirs was a true marriage. Yet Gail, despite her admiration for many of Burt's qualities, was not convinced that he was the best she could obtain. On the contrary, she assumed that one of these days, she would achieve a steady relationship with some lover, and then, by mutual consent, she and Burt would divorce each other and she would be free for another marriage.

In the meantime, she pursued her life of promiscuity as Burt did his, except that she was somewhat emotionally involved with each male, and he was not. And, as a result, each terminated affair left her desolate, though not as much as before the alliance with Burt. She would have a period of depression for a while, and then she would get into a new affair, which would run a course of anywhere from a night to several weeks, and then end.

During her periods of depression, Gail's intestines acted up, aggravating her ulcers. She came for therapy and it was soon clear that she was an emotionally dependent individual with a desperate need for love. Her anxiety and basic upset were related to this need.

Gail had the usual history found in these cases. Both her mother and father had been severely disturbed individuals who neglected her and made her a pawn in their own marital war. Finally, they separated, but not until Gail had been dragged between them for a number of years. Gail was technically placed in the custody of her mother; actually the child lived for long periods with an aunt who had five other children—the aunt certainly could not, or at least did not, give Gail much acceptance and approval.

Yes, I conceded, Gail had been sadly neglected but she had to understand there was nothing so "horrible and awful" about this. Neglect is the frequent lot of human beings. And although it would be better if children were *not* neglected by their parents and relatives, absence of neglect is not *necessary* for the development into happy human beings.

At first Gail was quite hostile to my ideas. She insisted she *did* need love, that every human being needs love, and that she was no exception to the rule. She strongly felt that unless

55

she was fully approved by her parents and by others there was no chance for happiness.

I refused to accept this and told her of several individuals, some of whom I knew and some of whom I took from her own life history, who were as unloved as she had been and who had still turned out fine.

I kept offering her material to prove that a human being does not have to be accepted either as a child or, later, as an adult, to be a happy, self-loving individual. I showed Gail that her best friend, a girl of her own age, Frances, had had a childhood which certainly was as bad as Gail's. Not only had Frances' parents been nasty to her when she lived with them, but finally, for no good reason, they had placed her in an orphanage though they were still living together. Frances, *even* though she had been abused by her parents and by practically everyone at the orphanage, was *not* an unhappy human being, did *not* have a dire need for love, and was getting along in life. Finally, though reluctantly, Gail began to see that her own unhappiness was not due only to the fact that she had been neglected as a child.

I also began to work with Gail on some of her current affairs—one in particular which she entered about five weeks after I began to see her—to show her that it was possible to be rejected and yet not conclude she was worthless. In this latest instance of rejection, her lover claimed at first to care for her a great deal, apparently to get her into bed (not realizing that she was persuadable without this line) and then, after sexual relations a few times, he made it clear he felt no love for her and wanted to see her only on a sexual basis. I made Gail see that although it was *sad* her lover felt this way, it was not horrible and catastrophic, and *she could well accept herself* despite the fact that he was interested only in her sexual ability.

After Gail and I worked through this and a few similar affairs, she began to realize she was not a horrible person just because the men she went with did not fully accept her. She became more and more confident as she saw herself as a separate entity in her own right, and she no longer needed the love of these men—Gail still wished to find a lover but her urge became more of a desire instead of a driving need.

When she was better able to accept herself, Gail thought of converting Burt to heterosexuality. She liked him, he was a good provider, a fine father to her child; she thought it might be possible, even though he was homosexual, to win him as a real sex partner. She knew she could not remain happily married to Burt—unless Burt could satisfy her sexually.

I told Gail that this was theoretically possible, since homosexuals are not born the way they are and can, and in some instances do, change remarkably, so that they can enjoy heterosexual activities. But I told her that Burt was not likely to change, because he did not consider himself disturbed. He insisted he thoroughly enjoyed his homosexual activities and showed no inclination whatever to come for therapy. Burt did come once to see me about Gail, but he made it clear he did not see himself as having need for therapy. He wanted to continue the relationship he had been having with Gail.

I explained the difficulties to Gail. If she wanted to try, there was nothing to be lost in attempting to seduce Burt into heterosexuality.

The two of us devised a plan of attack on Burt's heterosexual virginity. Since they did sleep together, the plan consisted largely of Gail's attempting, when Burt was in a reasonably good mood and when they were together in bed, to arouse him sexually.

Burt at first showed some irritation, then feigned indifference to her massaging his penis. But he seemed to get used to it, and even to like certain aspects after awhile. Then, to his surprise, on one occasion, he did achieve an erection as a result of her manipulating his genitals, and was able to have an orgasm. Thereafter he permitted her this, but practically no other kind of sexual activity.

After several months of successful oral-genital relations, Burt grew fond of Gail as a sex partner. Finally, Gail induced him to make an effort at penile-vaginal relations with her. Their first attempts were not very successful, but she was patient and showed no irritation or annoyance. At last he was able to have intercourse with her. Thereafter they achieved sex relations which seemed satisfactory to both of them.

In the meantime, Gail had lost interest in multiple male partners. While working to make Burt heterosexual, she only occasionally had affairs with other men—usually those who went out of their way to meet her. Her behavior was practically noncompulsive and relatively monogamous during this period. Then, when Burt began to satisfy her even more, she became completely monogamous, and was not interested, at least for the time, in other sex partners.

Burt, however, still was. He cut down his homosexual activities to every other week, while having sex relations with Gail two or three times a week. Soon, he had little objection to satisfying her sexually, even when he felt no real desire. But he did not give up his homosexuality.

Gail was disappointed. She had hoped Burt might become

a complete heterosexual. But I explained that he had his own problems, and was still not tackling his basic disturbances to any degree. There was no reason, therefore, to believe he would give up homosexuality. Now that he was having sex with males in a much less compulsive manner, his behavior was more in the normal range than previously. Gail had to face the fact that he would continue his homosexual activities.

By this time, Gail had come to like herself so much better, and had so little *compelling* need for love that she decided the relationship with Burt wasn't good enough. She would look for a more suitable man: a man who wanted her more than Burt did, and who was not homosexual. When she told Burt of her decision, he became so disturbed that he announced he would try harder—and apparently did.

When I last saw Gail, Burt was almost monogamous, having given up practically all his homosexual activity. Whether he would continue to do so was dubious, since he still had not attempted to solve any of his own problems. He was doing the right thing for the wrong reason. He was heterosexual because he did not want to lose Gail and the child that he loved so dearly. Though there was no certainty he would continue, for the time being he was behaving heterosexually.

Nevertheless, most homosexual-nymphomaniac matings do not have this ending—for several reasons. The people involved rarely come for therapy. They have usually chosen the mates they have, not because they wish to change their patterns, but because such mates will enable them to continue on the same pathways.

A homosexual doctor and a heterosexual and promiscuous nurse who met while he was interning, at a time when each had already embarked on constant man-hunting, decided to marry. They were not much concerned with teaming, their interest was in settling down. Their marriage has been sexless and childless, but they share their medical and business interests, and their common cultural and intellectual pursuits. Between them has grown a tremendous amount of personal affection and dependency. What makes the story important is that this is by no means unique. A college teacher of our acquaintance is married to a high school teacher; they have had their occasional sexual relations, but his erotic arousal is with other males—as is hers. Two children have come out of this marriage and, as one might easily predict, they are being

58

brought up in the strictest, most nonpermissive atmosphere.

We have also encountered another situation: a nymphomaniac, extremely disturbed, who keeps attaching herself, not to one male homosexual, but to an entire coterie of them, and particularly (though not always) to an effeminate group. Joan seems to like functioning without competition; and she perhaps enjoys the protective, motherlike role that she can play. In fact, in the homosexual groups, Joan is known as the queen mother. On rare occasions she will succeed in seducing one of her charges.

What can possibly be the motivation of two people to set up a *permanent* relationship: a highly-sexed heterosexual female and a highly-sexed homosexual male? Can it be a satisfactory partnership, an adjustment that has much to offer either or both of the parties?

1. Both the homosexual and the nymphomaniac partner are often motivated by the loneliness and despair that haunt the lives of those who enter innumerable sexual liaisons and are unable to solidify any of them. This is particularly true of the male homosexual (much less so of the lesbian), and it is largely true of the nymphomaniac. Rightly or wrongly, each sees in the partner-changing and in the varietist life a dissolute promiscuity; they think of it as a dead-end. "Where can it lead?" they ask themselves—and they are overwhelmed by the fear that it leads nowhere. In spite of all the marital unhappiness around them, *they believe in the romantic ideal,* think that they can be Héloise and Abelard, Romeo and Juliet, and they hope that everlasting bliss awaits them—if only this romantic love can be found.

If marriage is to be nonsexual (or only slightly sexual) and if it is to be childless (as in most of these instances), why need it include a male and female, and why the pretense of legal mating? This is a culturally induced feature. Unless there are very strong forces in the culture weighing upon a union to bind it—forces that are legal, psychological, social, economic, and even imaginary—that union tends to be easily disrupted. And our society exerts pressure on male-female unions to keep them intact, but never on male-male or female-female alliances.

2. What may start out as a marriage of convenience, often develops into one of affection. It is entirely possible, as sexual relations develop between the two persons, that each will find that searching elsewhere is unnecessary. One couple,

59

where the male was homosexual and the female lesbian before marriage, experimented sexually with each other and found the relationship so satisfactory that each relinquished their extramarital sexual affairs (Ellis, 1963f).

Particularly when the marriage is accompanied by counseling or therapy, it is possible for a formerly compulsive and promiscuous male homosexual and a formerly compulsive and promiscuous female heterosexual to minimize their adulterous interests, reduce their own tensions and anxieties, and to develop a more satisfactory image of themselves and of each other. However, a marriage of this type, *unaccompanied by therapy*, is generally doomed to failure, no matter how good the intentions of the partners.

3. It is possible that some homosexual husbands are held in low esteem by their promiscuous wives and it is likely, if not almost certain, that the corollary is often true. The homosexual male tends to dislike women, particularly "loose" women, "sexy" women. And the highly-sexed woman certainly has no respect for a male who is not interested in women. Each of the parties in this kind of marriage is able to lord it over the other; each may have an underlying need to choose a mate whom he (or she) holds in contempt.

4. Despite the fact that one spouse is same-sex, and the mate other-sex, oriented, each may be able to understand and accept the other. The compulsively promiscuous woman knows what it means to be driven by an imperious and uncontrollable urge to approach men. She has this feeling, and can understand it in another. The same is true of the male. Despite the underlying conventional moral standards found in many male homosexuals, they will often be heard to say, "If I were a girl, I'd really have a time of it. I'd go after every guy there is." Feeling this way, they are able to relate to a woman who does exactly that.

5. Precisely because there is sexual understanding that is ultra-permissive, and because there are no sexual demands made of each other, a homosexual-nymphomaniac marriage may have a better than average chance of endurance.

Few factors are so conducive to marital discord as jealousy. In the modern world, millions of married partners live in constant fear, haunted by the fantasy that the mate is lusting after another person—or is actually participating in some adulterous relationship. Judged rationally, the lust or even the overt infidelity of one's spouse may be entirely devoid of love, and may offer no threat of a disruption of the marriage. But partners in marriage are seldom able to judge these things objectively.

Given, however, a situation in which jealousy could not normally arise, and in which sexual incompatibility is unlikely to hinder the marriage, the union of a homosexual and a nymphomaniac may be free of two of the factors that most frequently cause American marriages to topple.

Despite possibilities that may exist for some element of gratification and success, marriage of a nymphomaniac and a homosexual is ill-advised, for several reasons:

1. It is unlikely to resolve the basic problem (especially, the low self-esteem), of which homosexuality and nymphomania are merely symptoms. *These problems require intensive therapeutic help.*

2. It is likely to be a marriage of neurotic interaction in which difficult personalities, not in gear, are each encouraging an aggravation of the defects and anxieties in the other.

3. It is usually a marriage in which the individuals pursue activities in which they see themselves, and each other, as degraded. The difficulty of achieving high esteem for a marriage in which each party has a low regard of himself and the other is almost insurmountable.

4. In a culture in which conventional behavior is so different from the behavior of the parties to the marriage, it is likely that disturbed children will be reared.

It is possible, however, with nymphomaniac-homosexual matings, to do something psychotherapeutically for either or both of the participants so they can get along together and can achieve a good heterosexual relationship. This is especially true if *both* partners are willing to come for therapy. In the case of Gail and Burt, the only therapeutic case of which we have first-hand knowledge, a reasonable degree of sexual and emotional compatibility was achieved—but the final outcome is still in doubt.

The fact remains that marriage between a nymphomaniac and a homosexual is difficult to maintain. It involves two disturbed individuals; and, in the great majority of instances, these people make a special kind of neurotic adjustment rather than face the fact that they are disturbed and require intensive psychotherapy. Therefore, these matings, although they may benefit the individuals involved, rarely wind up satisfactorily. They constitute a unique aspect of the nymphomaniac problem, and shed interesting sidelights on the question of nymphomania.

8

Induced Nymphomania

CAN THE SEXUAL DRIVES OF MEN AND WOMEN BE
heightened by the intake of drugs, foods, or alcoholic bever-
ages—or by hypnosis? Can a man or a woman be motivated
toward undesirable acts, under such influences?

For centuries, people have been fascinated by the subject
of aphrodisiacs. There is a vast folklore and mythology of
women who turned from frigid to passionate because of some
exotic plants they had eaten.

It has been amply demonstrated (MacDougald, 1955,
1961) that most of these reports cannot be scientifically true;
that the foods or other supposed aphrodisiacs can, in most
instances, have no effect other than mild suggestion. Lower
animals can be excited, by odor, to a point where they are
almost uncontrollable in their sexual interests. In fact, pseu-
dopregnancies have been induced in mice by purely olfactory
effects. But even the finest perfume in the world does little
more for a woman than to make her more desirable. It does
not create a drive that would otherwise be absent, nor does it
magnify a drive to uncontrollable dimensions (as perfume
advertising would suggest).

In a report of aphrodisiacs, MacDougald states:

> ... in spite of their vast popularity, almost no scien-
> tific studies have been written about them, since most
> of the writings on the subject are little more than un-
> scientific compilations of traditional material. According-
> ly, most beliefs about the subject are not based on the
> actual physiological facts involved.

One exception is of course *alcohol*, which MacDougald
describes as effecting "narcotization of the high inhibitory
senses and a dilation of the blood vessels." The popular
image of the heavy drinker as a promiscuous woman, fre-

quently having sexual affairs in a state of inebriation, *is not entirely untrue.*

In the case of alcoholism and nymphomania, we are dealing primarily not with cause and effect, but with two phenomena that may feed upon each other. The indiscriminate woman, who sees herself as uncontrollably promiscuous, will, in our society, usually have a low image of herself. She will regard her sexual activities *and her whole being* in a denigrating manner. She may have taken to alcohol for the same reason that she came to uncontrolled sexuality: unresolved neurotic problems, and their causes. But even if this were not the case, once she has become immersed in what is to her mind a worthless life, she may seek an outlet for her guilt in drink.

We may overestimate the frequency of alcoholism and female promiscuity, like that of alcoholism and male homosexuality, because of the few instances in our experience which stand out. If we know women who are both alcoholic and promiscuous, we are likely to link the two phenomena.

It would seem that alcohol does not increase a female's sex drive, *but it often decreases the fears and inhibitions* that accompany it. Here again there is an analogy with homosexuality; many writers have commented on liquor "bringing out" homosexual tendencies in men who are completely disinterested in other men when they are sober. A couple of shots of straight Scotch, and years of defenses are torn down.

Lolli (1961) tells of a woman who found it difficult to be responsive to her second husband, although she had responded to her first:

> Susan discovered that alcohol would help her to attain a reaction of the type welcomed by her husband. She also reinterpreted her past sexual life as inadequate. But she often had to trespass into the territory of inebriety in order to achieve the state desired by her husband. Eventually a body-mind unitary pleasure became inextricably woven into her sexual experiences and led to an addictive pattern of drinking.

In this case, although there is no problem of promiscuity or infidelity, Susan uses alcohol to diminish the socially induced barriers to sexual activity.

Lolli points out that there is little doubt "that the female addictive drinker is more ostracized socially and by the family than her male counterpart." Women, he insists, link

63

the onset of their drinking careers with some crucial event in their lives, such as a miscarriage, a divorce, an unhappy love affair, or the end of a happy job.

In the case of the nymphomaniac, we suggest that it may be the end of the image of self-respect that brings about the addictive drinking. *But the drinking does not induce the sexual activities,* although it may reduce some self-imposed restrictions against them.

Even less is known about sex activities that occur under the influence of hypnosis. Hypnosis has been practiced by amateurs, vaudevillians, charlatans, and the like for centuries. On the other hand, particularly during recent decades, it has been practiced by psychotherapists, obstetricians, dentists, and others who utilize it in an ethical, scientific manner. The first group, however, has contained many able technicians who are capable of putting individuals into a deep trance and who have attempted to induce these individuals to perform acts that they would otherwise be unwilling or unable to do. Some acts of sexual intercourse may have been performed under these circumstances, although reports of this type are practically never confirmed. At the same time, experimental, and clinical hypnotists, interested in aiding their patients, have utilized hypnosis to get them to talk about their sex lives, and have employed it to treat cases of frigidity.

There is a homily often repeated at hypnosis seminars to the effect that an unwilling female *cannot* be seduced by means of hypnosis; if the female is willing, the hypnosis is superfluous. As a generalization, that may be largely true; although vigorous sexual *suggestion,* short of inducing the girl into a trance, has frequently been known to be helpful to a would-be seducer. This, however, is not hypnosis.

Furthermore, hypnosis would not lead to nymphomania, because its effects largely end with the period of trance. Hypnosis has had only slight influence on the behavior patterns of normal people during their posthypnotic or "waking" state. Even if a hypnotized girl were to desire and to participate in sexual episodes, she could not be considered a nymphomaniac unless she had unquenchable and uncontrollable interests that *continued* to drive her to new sex experiences. Whatever else may be said of the relationship between hypnosis and the sex life of the subjects, *no such case* of hypnotically induced nymphomania has ever been reported.

When we turn our attention from alcoholic drinks and

64

temporary hypnotic trances to yohimbine and LSD, hashish and mescaline, we find a group of powerful drugs, many known for centuries and others synthesized only in recent years, whose effect upon the mind, nervous system, and sexual behavior man is only beginning to investigate.

It has been suggested that female hypereroticism, sometimes indiscriminate in its choice, may be induced in some individuals by certain of these drugs; while other drugs have the effect either of depressing the sex drive or of actually causing the individual to have difficulty reaching orgasm. This inability may, in the male, result in a prolonged sex act which offers heightened pleasures, except at the point where it induces anxiety about the unconcluded act; in the female, it may result in frequent desire for repetition of the act, with the same partner or others: hence, *unquenchability*, nymphomania.

According to a private communication from R. E. L. Masters, who is presently studying this problem, drugs apparently produce such hypereroticism in some persons by acting in at least four, more or less distinct, ways: (1) inhibitions are dissolved; (2) erotic fantasies occur which excite the individual and lead to an acting-out of the fantasies (as with *opium* or *hashish*); (3) genital engorgement is produced, with resulting urgent desires (as with *santonin* or *cocaine*); (4) amoralization of the individual occurs and desires are immediately gratified, without thought of consequence—as with various of the *Solanaceae* derivatives.

The derivatives of *Solanaceae* have for centuries been considered powerful erotic stimulants, able to induce hypereroticism. These drugs are derived from such plants as thorn apple, belladonna, mandragora, and the henbanes. They contain the alkaloids atropine, hyoscyamine, and scopolamine, among others, and are said to produce extreme confusion and demoralization, and to result in promiscuous behavior by otherwise restrained individuals. They are also reported to have induced "deviant" non-coital sexual practices.

Amnesia of what has occurred, accompanied by severe depression, rather commonly follow in the wake of the intoxication and of the sexual activities.

These were the drugs presumably dispensed at the orgiastic gathering of heretical sects and of "witches" from about the middle of the fifteenth through the middle of the eighteenth centuries; but, in dealing with events of that time, one cannot be sure of the recorder's ability to differentiate truth from hyperbole, or to know whether the effects described (if they did actually occur) were induced by the drugs or by the

65

hysterical atmosphere that pervades some religious groups. A French scholar and historian, who wrote prolifically on women, love, sex, and other subjects (Michelet, 1939), tells of a gathering of "witches" in which the *Solanaceae* derivatives were used to produce near-paralysis in a husband and nymphomania in his wife. According to Michelet, the man had to look on helplessly while his usually faithful wife, "reduced to a deplorable state of self-abandonment, would ... be shown him naked and unashamed ... enduring the caresses of another." One cannot but wonder whether the *surroundings* and the knowledge of the drugs' potentialities did not produce a sort of hypnotic state that would have had the same results if the man and his wife had been given placebos.

In a more recent document (Hesse, 1946), which relies on older sources, the writer paraphrases Riebling, who had encountered such a case resulting from an accidental atropine-scopolamine intoxication:

A fifty-four-year-old-woman ... inadvertently took too many atropine-scopolamine drops. During her narcotic psychosis, she attempted to have a lesbian intercourse with her landlady, and unashamedly she invited also the fiancé of the landlady to have sexual intercourse with her. After her recovery from the intoxication, she had no memory of all these happenings.

The *Solanaceae* drugs were formerly used rather commonly in the treatment of asthma patients, although they have recently been replaced by other agents. During the period of their use, there were many reports, always difficult to confirm, of erotic imagery, sometimes with considerable sexual stimulation, that might have led to behavioral excesses.

The *Solanaceae* traditionally have been used by the Arabs, often in combination with hashish, for the purpose of inducing intense erotic activities in both males and females. There is a vast folklore about hashish as an aphrodisiac, but little of it is scientifically acceptable at this point.

Nymphomania, and behavior akin to it, are reported by many writers to be induced by *cocaine;* but there is some question as to whether the accounts are not exaggerated by romanticists and by moralists, or whether there is a concomitant development of interest in sexual abandonment and drugs. That more than one of these factors can simultaneously be at play, interacting in such a manner as to bring about

66

enhanced effects, is indicated in another study (Finch, 1960):

There is removal (after taking cocaine) of normal inhibitions with increased erotic tension in women, characterized by marked engorgement and congestion of the genital organs. It appears that these erotic reflexes occur chiefly in the woman ... With the excitement of the brain, sexual desires loom up to the fore. In men there is increased sexual desire with erotic ideas developing into perversions which are carried even to the extent of violence. With women the same sexual stimulation occurs, but erotic manifestations are more marked, with a tendency to produce complete loss of moral sense and nymphomania.

That cocaine must here be differentiated from *heroin* and other drugs is emphasized by one authority (De Ropp, 1957). The popular notion of the dope fiend, he suggests may be derived from the behavior of the cocainist, and then falsely applied to heroin addicts.

In addition to the traditional aphrodisiacs, there are many varieties of drugs that are said to produce sexual excitement in some persons, but no controlled experiments have been made that indicate this enhanced sexual interest would not have been induced by a harmless placebo. There are any number of drugs that are stimulants, just as there are depressants, and such stimulants of the sympathetic nervous system may cause sexual excitement. It is hardly likely that this could lead to continued excitement (as in nymphomania) or overpowering and uncontrollable abandon. Marijuana, damiana, nanacatl, bufotenin, ololiugui, the opium derivatives heroin and morphine, the tonka bean, and some tranquilizers are said to have yielded such intense excitement and activity. However, the extent to which a woman is made hypererotic would depend upon her emotional and physical condition, the elements of suggestion and expectation, and neurotic or psychotic predispositions.

A male who has used opium, mescaline, LSD, and other drugs has written to one of the authors as follows:

Sexual intercourse (including fellatio, cunnilingus, and sodomy) during opium intoxication may be so intensely pleasurable an experience that the individual will be uncontrolled in seeking to re-experience the intoxication and indulge in intercourse with whatever partner or partners may be at hand. Not only may erotic visions produce excitation, but the gentials sometimes feel unusually and pleasurably engorged, while a mild anesthesia at once guarantees prolongation of the act and heightens voluptuousness.

Similar reports have been forthcoming from users of *heroin* and *morphine*, particularly from individuals not severely addicted. Long-term addiction to opium or its derivatives, it is reported, usually results in diminished desire and pleasure.

Effects similar to those described for opium have been reported for the hallucinogenic drugs, such as *LSD-25, psilocybin,* and *mescaline.* Erotic visions may occur, and individuals may seize upon the heightened capacity for concentration afforded by these drugs to produce vivid and intricate erotic fantasies which the individual may then crave to act out, and may actually do so. Especially with LSD, there may be a regression to an infantile state wherein immediate gratification of appetites and wishes will be demanded. There have been some verbal reports by those taking drugs (which may be exaggerations, but which may on the other hand be confirmable—but not yet reduced to writing because of the social atmosphere) that nymphomania-like and satyriasis-like behavior have been induced by the hallucinogens. Such behavior will continue only during the period of influence of the drug, and when the subject behaves in a manner considered dangerous by the experimenter, the drug intoxication may be swiftly terminated by a counteragent.

Preliminary data on the sexual effects of the hallucinogens has been provided by R.E.L. Masters (personal communication) who has not in all instances witnessed the reaction, but reports cases later related to him by people who took them. Among the cases he cites is that of a female who, alone in her apartment, experienced mescaline intoxication with hypereroticism resulting when she "concentrated on sex." The girl was, however, deterred from putting her desire into practice because, she stated, she did not wish to have relations with a male who was not sharing the drug experience. She hoped that an intruder would break into her apartment and assault her—a fantasy that certainly reflects an imagination that has lost contact with reality.

The picture remains confused. Many who have taken the hallucinogens, and others who have observed them, have declared these drugs to be sex depressants (that is, anti-aphrodisiacs or anaphrodisiacs). Gerald Heard (1963), who writes subjectively of his own experiences with LSD-25, is enthusiastic about its effect on fantasy, imagination, and consciousness. However, Heard is completely negative in his description of the effect on libido: "Any sexual sensation, any erotic fantasy or preoccupation, is nearly always reported as absent."

The Food and Drug Administration at one time reported that teenage sex orgies were resulting from a consumption of a combination of two *secobarbital* capsules and one *benzedrine* tablet.

Nevertheless, it is difficult to establish that the teenage girls had an enhanced desire for sex activity or that they had fewer inhibitions. The girls were apparently part of a rebellious youth group that would in general be drug-oriented and kicks-oriented.

Recently, there was a report of a black market in a drug with the trade name of Exitana (which may be an orthographic error: Excitana?), made from the root of a jungle plant in Brazil. Nymphomania in the female and priapism in the male are the reported effects. One informant writes that "a wave of rapes and orgies in Latin America was attributed to the drug." The history of the folklore of aphrodisiacs makes one skeptical, but it is not outside the realm of scientific possibility.

One final type of induced nymphomania may here be mentioned: the so-called "epidemics of erotomania" that were said to have occurred among nuns during the seventeenth century, particularly in French convents. Undoubtedly, these women were hysterics; they were able to give vent to their suppressed sexual needs, and at the same time retain their religiosity, by believing that they were possessed by evil spirits or by the devil (Huxley, 1952; Masters, 1962a, 1962b).

It usually happened that one nun would become possessed, would infect others, and finally most or all of the nuns would be affected. At Loudon, where the Ursuline convent was located, this occurred with such frequency that it was said to have become a major tourist attraction for many years.

If indeed these were hysterical phenomena, brought on by pathological autosuggestion, then similar hysteria might be induced by drugs, by hypnosis, or by other means.

One other group of drugs may result in enhanced female libido, namely the *sex hormones;* and particularly, "it is the male sex hormone that has been found to be most effective in enhancing libido in the female" (Kupperman, 1961). Although many patients expressed the information that their sex drives and interests have been increased by sex hormones, Kupperman suggests their use (oral, parenteral, or topical) normally does not bring on insatiable and uncontrollable sex urges. On the other hand, large doses of male hormone given regularly to females may lead to exceptionally strong sex urges. In a medical article "Drugs Influencing Sexual Desire and Performance," in *Medical Letter on Drugs and Therapeutics* (June 7, 1963), it is pointed out that "testosterone propionate, when given to women in larger doses (100 to 200 mg., three times a week), causes intensified and often distressing libido and genital sensitivity, together with signs of virilization. Although some clinicians use smaller doses of androgens in the treatment of frigidity, there is little evidence of more than placebo effects, and there is no evidence that use of a single 'aphrodisiac' dose has any effect."

Significantly, some hormones (particularly the androgens) are actually used in the treatment of nymphomania. Kupperman explains this paradox as follows:

> Those patients exhibiting nymphomania who respond to androgens by a decrease in desire for repeated sexual contacts are probably women who have been attempting these many sexual contacts without deriving sexual gratification owing to failure to achieve an orgasm. The addition of androgens helps them to achieve an orgasm, thereby accomplishing gratification so that an excessive number of sexual contacts is no longer necessary.

With this morass of contradictory and tentative evidence, amid the folklore and the rumors and the gossip, what can be said about induced nymphomania? We suggest that the following emerges:

1. Most of the folklore must be discounted, until it is confirmed or disconfirmed in the future by good scientific evidence. In the meantime, it throws more light on the cultures which create these narrations than on the events that are narrated.

2. There are several drugs that reduce an individual's resistance or inhibition to sex activities. Alcohol and certain other drugs may, therefore, lessen obstacles to nymphomania, even though they will not actually induce nymphomaniacal behavior.

3. Some drugs, including alcohol, are taken by people who are disturbed about their activities. In such instances, the

drugs do not induce nymphomania, but if anything, a woman's shame over her compulsive promiscuity may well bring on alcohol or drug addiction.

4. Nymphomania may be a symptom of a deep disturbance, of which alcoholism or drug addiction may be another such symptom. The two kinds of addictions may be concomitants, rather than cause and effect, and they then should be looked upon as parts of one syndrome.

5. While behavior that a woman ordinarily would resist can and does take place under the influence of some external agent (drug, hypnotist, etc.), it is unlikely that this pattern or behavior would persist when she is no longer under the direct influence of such an agent. Since nymphomania involves repeated, patterned, and unquenchable drive, it would not normally be inducible under these conditions.

6. Sex hormones, hallucinogens, stimulants, and other chemical agents may have a profound effect on the bodies and minds of people, including the sex drive. Although no authenticated cases of induced nymphomania or female erotomania have been traced to these agents, scientific experimentation in this area has only begun, and may yield interesting data in the near future.

Note: The writers are indebted to Mr. R. E. L. Masters for calling to our attention some of the above references, and for making available certain of the information in this chapter. However, Mr. Masters is not responsible for any of the comments or analyses made, nor is he responsible for the material gathered from the authors' experience and from other sources.

PART THREE

Causes

9

The Mystique of Nymphomania

DESPITE THE ALMOST INNUMERABLE STUDIES AND RE-ports of sex activities that have appeared during the past decades, only slight attention has been focused on the compulsively promiscuous woman. This is probably a result of the relative infrequency of nymphomania, the ease with which it can be concealed, and the confusion which exists about the definitions of nymphomania, prostitution, and promiscuity; it may also result from the fact that most of this research is done by males. Until recently, women played no role in such studies, other than as subjects; and the men who wrote the major works of sexology generally saw women as undersexed. The beast in the jungle that was sex was to be found in the male; and he it was who was guilty of such undesirable activities as lust, seduction, rape, exhibitionism, sadism, and homosexuality.

On rare occasions, however, a case history has been reported of a woman who would, today, be called a nymphomaniac. In what was probably the first systematic study of sexual disorders in which the author utilized both medical literature and a relatively large number of case histories (Krafft-Ebing, 1922), the term hyperaesthesia was employed to describe "abnormally increased sexual desire." Falling back on the Darwinian theory of evolution, which was then popular for explaining almost any cultural or biological phenomenon, Krafft-Ebing suggested that hyperaesthesia is the outcome of the breeding of many centuries; hence, is an hereditary characteristic:

> It is fortunate for society and for the criminal doctor, who is called upon to make the diagnosis, that these cases, in which irresistible hypersensuality leads to the gravest and indisputably pathological sexual abberations, are only encountered in that category of human beings whom we class among the degenerates infected with hereditary taint.

Krafft-Ebing saw these hypersexually driven people as manic, and divided the manics into two groups: males suffering from satyriasis and females from nymphomania. The latter, he asserted, is not properly to be classified as a disease; nymphomania is "only a syndrome within the sphere of psychical degeneration." Some of the cases he cited are those of girls *literally* dying for sex.

One young girl, recently jilted by her fiancé, threw herself at men with maniacal lack of restraint. "She refused to put on her garments, had to be held down in bed by muscular men and furiously demanded coitus. Insomnia, congestion of the facial nerves, a dry tongue, and rapid pulse. Within a few days lethal collapse."

Krafft-Ebing reported other terminal cases: a "modest and decent" woman of thirty was "suddenly seized with an attack of nymphomania, unlimited desire for sexual gratification, obscene delirium." And again the verdict: "Death from exhaustion within a few days."

This type of case, of which Krafft-Ebing cites several, seems closer to hysteria than to what is today termed nymphomania. To differentiate the sudden seizures from an unceasing but recurrent sex drive, so strong that it is difficult to handle, Krafft-Ebing called the latter chronic nymphomania, stated that it was the more frequently encountered, and that it seemed "to occur only in individuals psychically degenerated." He found it to be the result of sexual hyperaesthesia, rather than synonymous with it, and pointed out some special aspects of its compulsivity. The condition, he noted, manifests itself in impulsive but not necessarily involuntary acts, "inasmuch as ethical considerations may counterbalance the milder forms of sexual excitement."

Thus we have one of the earliest descriptions of the dilemma of the woman who essentially accepts but cannot conform

73

to the dicta of an antisexual society. She has irresistible impulses that force her to sacrifice feminine "honor and dignity."

One of Krafft-Ebing's cases, Mrs. V., came from a good family. She was modest, good-natured, and blushed easily. But during her youth she was insatiable in her need for men; and she continued to lust after males when she was a grand-mother, finally attempting to seduce a twelve year old. This case was taken from a French medical journal, and was to become the oft-repeated classic of the nineteenth century. It is given in detail later in this chapter.

Another case reported by Krafft-Ebing is that of Mrs. E., who came from a "tainted" family. Her paternal uncle was insane, her father was oversexed, and she herself was nervous and eccentric. Her first sexual intercourse took place when she was ten; and, after she married at the age of nineteen, she continued her sexual activities with many men. Mrs. E. described her own condition as "monomania for men," and, from all indications, it was not only the uncontrollable nature of her desires, but the conflicts created by her self-contempt for giving in to these desires, that put her condition in the nymphomania category. "Fully conscious of the abominable nature of her conduct, she was powerless in restraining her insatiable appetite."

Soon after the clinical reports of Krafft-Ebing were published, there appeared the first studies of Freud and his followers. Freud largely depicted hysterical women as those who had repressed or unsuccessfully sublimated their high sexual energies. It was with the work of Havelock Ellis, however, that attention was again turned to the problems of women who were fulfilling their sexual interest, rather than suppressing it.

Havelock Ellis dealt only slighly with cases of nymphomania, most of which he culled from previous literature in an effort to determine whether the condition could be correlated with any physiological manifestations. In one study (Ellis, 1936) he offers a suggestion as to the origin of the word:

If we take a wider view of the psychic place of water in the history of civilization, it would appear that at many of the chief places of origin of the higher human cultures—Egypt, India, Persia, Greece—water was often regarded, by a premonition of the modern scientific view of the pelagic origin of life, as the source of all things. This belief was sometimes erotically tinged; Venus (Adadyomene) arose from the sea, and the classic nymphs had erotic associations, which are preserved and emphasized in the term nymphomania.

The scientific literature in the early part of the twentieth century dealt only to a slight extent with hypersexuality in women, although the word nymphomania began to appear regularly (occasionally intermixed with the terms erotomania or urethromania). A few cases were copied from one text to another, and the writers kept seeking concomitant physical signs of degeneration, either in the subject or in her family.

One of the earliest writers to make a comparison of the oversexed male and female, and to place this in the context of cultural attitudes toward the two, pointed out a prevalent attitude—that satyriasis was relatively rare, nymphomania more frequent—and rejected this, stating that it was an error derived from failure to take into account the normal sexual desire of women (Hühner, 1916):

When a single man has sexual desire he generally indulges in intercourse, and no notice is taken of the fact. But, under our present social conditions, an unmarried woman is supposed to suppress all thoughts of sexual intercourse, and so we have come to regard one who, teased by a strong (though still normal) sexual impulse, betrays it by her actions as a nymphomaniac. This condition, however, is not true nymphomania. In making our comparisons of the frequence of nymphomania as compared to satyriasis, we must take into account that the sufferer from satyriasis may remain undetected for a long time (in mild cases possibly for life) while the nymphomaniac is more readily recognized.

Hühner repeats many of the then-held myths of sex that seem today to be outdated to the point of incredibility (many of the nymphomaniacs were masturbators, for example). But he believed they are born, not made. They come from families in which there is insanity, and many of them end up in asylums. He notes that "every indulgence increases the desire and lessens the capacity [for gratification]." One case cited by Hühner is interesting because the affected female is *not* promiscuous; her overwhelming insatiable desire can be channelized exclusively toward her husband:

The patient lived happily with her husband until after the birth of her first child. From that moment insatiable

75

lust seized her. An irresistible craving suddenly took hold of her—an indomitable lust to embrace a man. In her genitals she felt a morbid itching, an inexplicable excitement, a burning desire for sexual gratification. In the beginning her husband tried to satisfy her until he discovered his inability to do this. She did not allow an hour of the day to pass without demanding gratification from her husband.

But most instances cited by Hühner are not of this character. He notes the case cited by another authority (Lombroso, 1918), of a woman who surrendered herself to her husband's laborers, without discrimination; of another who had for her lovers "all the desperadoes of Texas," and another who had intercourse "with all the herdsmen of her village."

"What can be done with nymphomaniacs?" asks Hühner. Very little, he believes, except perhaps to put them in an asylum.

Outstanding among the serious researchers in sexual problems in Europe from the early part of the twentieth century until the rise of Hitler to power was Magnus Hirschfeld. Although Hirschfeld's greatest interests and contributions were in the field of homosexual behavior, he devoted attention to all types of anomalies and disorders. A collection of his writings on these subjects was made by his students and published posthumously in 1948. Hypererotism, or excessive sexuality, can only be considered in relation to one's definition of "normal" sexuality, Hirschfeld contends. He reported (as later did Kinsey and his associates) individuals who have had intercourse four or five times a day; others, 1000 times a year. Hirschfeld noted this would be extremely time-consuming but it would not be a disorder if the people involved could control their acts, indulge in them rationally, and did not have a low image of themselves because of their intensive sex drives.

Unfortunately, Hirschfeld sometimes confused men and women whose sexual drive did not appreciably diminish over a long period of time, with those whose drives were unquenchable. He defined hypereroticism as a state "represented by a degree of libido at which sexual desire reawakens immediately or shortly after sexual relief," but went on to state that this drive could be directed toward one or many persons, and be discriminate or indiscriminate, monogamous or polygamous. Many of the cases he described were those of highly sexed males, predominantly or almost exclusively interested in their mate, but seeking noncoital contact—which Hirschfeld considered abnormal.

In regard to polygamous hypererotic women, Hirschfeld pointed out that these nymphomaniacs "give themselves resistless and without discrimination to any man who accosts them in the street." Some of them, he noted, who suppress instead of express their urges, have coital hallucinations:

> These are always very hysterical women, who actually become ecstatic under the imaginary coitus; their uterus twitches and actually ejects the usual substance under the effect of an orgiastic sensation, exactly as in normal intercourse. Such paroxysms occur during sleep, in a state of intoxication, or in a hypnotic or narcotic condition, and they have actually led to unfounded charges of indecent manipulation and even rape against doctors, employers, and others.

"Uncontrollable erotomania" was briefly discussed by Feré 1932 who noted that it is accomplished by anguish. It is a pathological condition, he contended, more frequent among women than men. The erotomaniac is mad with inaccessible love; with amorous passion she chases the completely unattainable. Feré, although not documenting his material, had many insights remarkable for his time. For example: "But some of the more feeble [of the erotomaniacs] confine themselves to lamenting over their own unworthiness, which they endure with pious resignation." But much of his scientific work was diluted with moralizing: "In promiscuity, both men and women lose part of their moral and physical value, and their offspring are more liable to illness and death."

One of the most important sexologists in the early decades of the twentieth century was Iwan Bloch, many of whose works have been available in English, including his monumental: *The Sexual Life of our Time* (1908). Unlike Feré, Bloch contended that abnormal increase in sexual drive is more frequent in men than in women: "It may be permanent or periodic; it almost always arises from lascivious ideas." When these ideas seize the stricken individual, she may become sexually insane, and, "like the wild animals," rush at the first male she meets to gratify her lust. And what causes this? *Excessive masturbation,* Bloch says. He goes on to cite some cases. One woman would give herself, in a single day, to four or five different men. She asked every male who approached her to perform coitus with her.

Still another instance cited by Bloch comes from the

French medical press. It is worth quoting in detail here, because it is probably one of the few instances of an authenticated case of nymphomania reported by a medical authority previous to the twentieth century:

Madame V., of a strong constitution, agreeable exterior, good-natured manner, but very reserved, came under the care of Trelat on January 1, 1854. Notwithstanding the fact that she was sixty years of age, she still worked very diligently, and hardly spared herself time for meals. Nothing in her outward appearance or in her actions indicated during her stay in the asylum that she was in any way affected with mental disorder. During the four years not a single obscene word, not a gesture, not the slightest passionate movement, indicated anger or impatience.

Since her earliest years, she has pursued handsome men and given herself to them. When a young girl, by this degrading conduct she reduced her parents to despair. Of an amiable character, she blushed when anyone spoke a word to her. She cast her eyes down when in the presence of several persons; but as soon as she was alone with a young or old man, or even with a child, she was immediately transformed; she lifted her petticoats, and attacked with a raging energy him who was the object of her insane love.

In such moments she was a Messalina, whereas a few instants before one would have regarded her as a virgin. A few times she met with resistance, and received severe moral lectures, but far more often there was no obstacle to her desires. Although various distressing adventures occurred, her parents arranged for her marriage, in the hope thereby to put an end to the moral disturbance. But her marriage was only a new scandal. She loved her husband passionately; and she loved with the like passion every man with whom she happened to be alone; and she exhibited so much cunning and cleverness that she made a mock of any attempts at watching her, and often attained her end. Now it was a manual worker busy at his trade, now some one walking past her in the street, to whom she spoke, and whom she brought home with her on any possible excuse—a young man, a servant, a child, returning from school! In her exterior she appeared so blameless, and she spoke so gently, that every one followed her without mistrust. More than once she was beaten or robbed; but this did not prevent her from continuing the same way of life. Even when she had become a grandmother there was no change. One day she enticed a boy, twelve years of age, into her house, having told him that his mother was coming to see her. She gave him sweets, embraced and kissed him, and as she then began to take off his clothes and approached him with obscene gestures, the boy strove to resist her. He struck her, and he related everything to his brother, twenty-four years of age. The brother entered the house pointed out by the boy, and abused the corrupt woman to the uttermost.

She was shut up in a convent, where she behaved in so good, sweet, amiable, and modest a manner, that no one would have believed that she had ever committed the slightest fault, and representations were made to the effect that she ought to be allowed to return to her home. All the inmates of the convent had been charmed by the zeal with which she took part in the religious exercises. When she was free again, the scandalous doings were immediately resumed, and so it went all through her life.

After she had reduced her husband and children to despair, they finally hoped that age would extinguish the fire with which she was consumed. They were mistaken. The more excesses she committed, the more she wanted to commit, the more vigorous she appeared. It is hardly credible that such debased ideas and habits should leave intact such a sweet expression of countenance, a voice so youthful, a behavior so full of calm repose, and a glance of such clear assurance. She became a widow. Her children, on account of her horrible mode of life, could not any longer keep her at home, and they sent her to a distant place, where they provided her with an allowance. Since she was now old, she was at length compelled to offer payment for the shameful services which she demanded; and as the small allowance she received did not suffice for this purpose, she worked with untiring zeal in order to be able to pay the great number of her lovers.

To see the old, alert woman sitting at her work, as I myself saw her, when aged seventy or upwards, without spectacles, always cleanly and carefully, but not strikingly, dressed, with a simple and honorable appearance, and an open countenance—to suspect her shameful mode of life would never occur to anyone. Several of the wretched men who were paid by her related how diligent she was. She assured Trelat of her morality, in the hope that he would discharge her, and so enable her to resume her mode of life. Trelat could not agree to this, and he succeeded in obtaining from one of the men an accurate account of her shameless loves.

This corrupt woman preserved her repose of manner, her excellent appearance, and her honorable demeanor until her death. She died at the age of seventy-four years from a cerebral hemmorrhage. There was no remarkable change in the brain.

Although devoid of any investigation into the background of the condition, and replete with moralizing remarks, this remains one of the best descriptions of nymphomania in the early literature of sexology. The woman was compulsive and uncontrollable; she was indiscriminate and often irrational.

Up to a few years ago, there were frequent references to nymphomania in the technical literature, and an occasional case history, but few enlightened analyses. Despite their moralistic remarks, sexologists did differentiate between nymphomania and *controlled* promiscuity. But they were at a loss as to the origin of the compulsive hypersexuality of nymphomania, and thought that its treatment consisted of bromides, change of clothing, or institutionalization. Sexology at the time had to fight enormous prejudices; among others, a social outlook that denied the existence of sexual desires to any decent woman.

When, however, in later years, clinicians and students of human sexual behavior started to discover large numbers of women who participate in sex acts with more than one man, before or after their marriages, they began to differentiate these from females who were uncontrollable and irrational in their promiscuity. The groundwork was then begun for a more enlightened definition of nymphomania.

With the work of Havelock Ellis, Freud, Adler, Reich, Jung and others, the Western world found itself in the midst of a sexual revolution, leading to a flood of publications, the best-known and most influential indubitably being the first two volumes of the Institute for Sex Research, popularly known as the Kinsey reports of 1948 and 1953. Research on sex behavior became almost respectable, grants were given for it, studies were made in prisons, in universities, and of church members—and sex publications became so abundant that a bibliography of the serious and important works would include hundreds of entries.

Sex began to be studied and written about from the viewpoint of almost every discipline. Almost every aspect of sex activities has by now been studied with some seriousness: the sex life of the infant, of the adolescent, of the college student, of the aged; the sex life of the criminal, of the narcotic addict, of the alcoholic; and the patterns of those participating in incestuous behavior, in male and female homosexual relationships, in sadistic and masochistic activities.

Yet, little has yet been written on nymphomania. Rarely does a case study appear; the phenomenon is, in fact, prominent by its absence from otherwise rather comprehensive works. For example, when one of the writers co-edited a two-volume encyclopedia of sex (Ellis and Abarbanel, 1961), no separate entry for nymphomania was included—the word appears in the lengthy and detailed index with but a single page entry.

Why the paucity of studies in this field? Perhaps it is because *nymphomania* has been used loosely—to describe the sexually awakened woman, rather than the compulsively promiscuous woman. The former is usually not driven to therapy, except when she accepts and internalizes society's condemnation of her and, consequently, develops a feeling of self-worthlessness. Usually, however, the promiscuous woman does not bring herself to the therapist. When she does, it is often for reasons other than her sex life (one example, Gail with her ulcers, is reported in a previous chapter).

Nevertheless, although the literature on nymphomania continues to be meager, here and there a serious report on the nymphomaniac has appeared. One such case study is described by the distinguished British sexologist, Clifford Allen (1949), whose works reflect an authenticity not always found in sex studies. Allen finds that hypersexuality is rare in man, still less common in woman. Oversexed women appearing in legend may be regarded, he believes, as wish-fulfilling fantasies because so many women have, in actuality, been frigid and unresponsive. He suggests numerous possible causes for the hypersexuality: that the woman may be to some extent homosexual, leading her to seek an "active" rather than a "passive" role with men; that she is seeking a "father-surrogate, and her intense sexual urge is unconsciously incestuous"; or that there are physical reasons, including the inability to achieve orgasm. He describes one case briefly:

> The writer has seen a hypomanic girl who developed her very mild psychosis following adrenalectomy. How far her condition was endocrine and how far psychogenic it was impossible to say. She had previously been a quiet, well-behaved girl who lived a stable, perhaps monotonous, life with her parents. When she developed the hypomania and sexual hyperversion she started to use cosmetics excessively and to be exhibitionistic—lying about on the lawn where she could be seen clad in the briefest of "sun-suits." She spent much of her time telephoning young men with whom she sometimes had had the slightest of acquaintanceship, and leading the conversation into channels of sex and marriage. Finally she enticed a young student into becoming engaged to her and, although he was studying theology, soon seduced him. It was with some difficulty and considerable sedation that she was tided over this illness but she finally recovered and behaved normally. The exact reason why excessive sexual feeling should be associated with mania is not known, but no doubt the excitement, and exultation of feeling, combined with the increased metabolism of manic states have a great deal to do with it.

From the brief account of this patient, one cannot be at all sure that hypersexuality is involved. That she underwent physiological changes that induced behavioral changes, producing anxiety, seems evident. But the alteration in her personality may have been from shyness to an obsession with sex and marriage, and a compulsive urge to induce a man to copulate with her, who, for religious reasons, may have been as fearful and repressed as she had formerly been herself. Two factors, do, however, make the case of interest: the strong probability that the behavioral changes were induced by *physiological* conditions (the adrenalectomy), and the self-condemnation that accompanied the changes. The patient evidently defined her condition as a disease and therefore, for her, it was a disease.

In still another study (Allen, 1962) the writer discussed a compulsively promiscuous woman who was *unable to achieve orgasm;* for many researchers, these are the only women who are described under the heading of nymphomania.

A popular study written by the physician L. T. Woodward (1961), deals with the use of *hypnosis* in the treatment of sexually disturbed men and women. Among the cases described are the impotent, the frigid, the homosexual, and one woman who was compulsively promiscuous. Although Woodward warns that hypnosis is not a short-cut or a cure-all, he does make it appear that at least the nymphomaniac overcame her problem without too much difficulty, once he had set her on the right path.

In Woodward's case history, Joanne came to him after ten months of orthodox Freudian therapy. She felt she was getting nowhere, and was deeply distressed about her sex life. "Why do you feel so guilty about sex?" she was asked. She replied:

Because—because it's so compulsive. I'd like to have the choice, the freedom to have sex or not have it. I'm not the sort who believes a girl ought to be a virgin until she marries. Not at all. I think it's a good idea for a girl to get some sex experience. But not to become a nympho. Not to take on everybody who makes a pass at her.

Joanne described some of her experiences, and seemed anxious to do so in the most self-condemnatory manner.

You ought to hear about some of the men I've slept with. Your hair would curl, Doctor. Drunks, filthy tramps. Old pot-bellied men in their sixties and even older. Bellhops. Kids of fifteen. Slick greasy-haired pimps. The most revolting kind of people.

Woodward, like several others, draws the distinction between the woman who achieves orgasm and the woman who does not; the former he never defines as a nymphomaniac. Joanne having experienced orgasms with normal frequency, Woodward places her into another category: a girl of compulsive promiscuity. And she was a girl who needed love and acceptance; who saw herself, in her adolescence, as being scholarly but physically unattractive, and utilized sex to get the boys to chase her.

Many interesting aspects of the case were probed by Woodward: attachment to a father, flight from repressed lesbianism, need to love and to be loved. Hypnosis was utilized for two purposes: to probe repressed memories, and to place her under posthypnotic influence in which she would (temporarily, the author emphasizes) find physical contact with men repulsive, and hence be able to refuse them. What evidently aided Joanne to work out her problems may have been the healthy, nonmoralistic attitude of the therapist, even more than did the hypnotic suggestion. For Woodward writes:

> I pointed out to her that by her own moral standards there was nothing wrong with occasional sex experiences; it was the compulsive, involuntary sex acts that were neurotic. She soon saw that she was giving herself only to men she cared for, and refusing those who did not interest her.

Like so many men and women who appear in case studies (which, unfortunately, tell us much more about the successes of therapy than of the failures), Joanne married, had children, and it is assumed had no recurrence of her difficulties. Nevertheless, it is disconcerting to read the story of Joanne side by side with another work by the same author, *The Deceivers* (Woodward, 1962), in which he is moralistic about the sex lives of many women. The "deceivers" are the adulterers in American society, particularly in Suburbia, and we are introduced to one, Doris, a highly-sexed woman who had taken to masturbation in her search for gratification. Doris describes the seduction of a delivery boy who had come to the house with groceries:

> She knew that she was acting insanely, wickedly, Doris told me. But she found it impossible to control herself.

> "I don't know what that poor boy must have thought," she said. "He was only fourteen, you know. We were in the kitchen, so I took his hand and led him to the bedroom. But he didn't know exactly what to do. He just stood there, sort of gulping and blushing. I told him to take his shoes off, which he did. Then I made him sit on the edge of the bed."

> "You realized the wrong you were doing? This was practically a child," I said.

But the lad, evidently filled with excitement and fear, was not overly concerned with the wrong that was being done to him. He had a premature ejaculation, and when this was related to Woodward, he said to Doris: "So it came to nothing. The wages of sin."

Probably the most detailed story of a nymphomaniac that has been recorded, although more descriptive than analytic, is *Diary of a Nymph,* by Nathan Shiff (1961). The author is a physician and psychiatrist, and the book consists largely of tape recordings of his patient. Christine is not only compulsive, she is basically antisexual. She describes sex as "filthy and cheap," she wants to mingle "with sane and decent people." She has a need to "talk and talk till I feel clean again..." and to feel that "whatever I ever did that was filthy and low wasn't really me doing it, the real me I've always had a notion of." She wanted to be outside her own body, as if the real Christine was "a moral person, the respectable wife." To which she adds, in a self-mocking but self-revelatory note: "[when out on a date] there was a part of me reacting more like a Sunday school miss than a call girl."

Christine is a classic self-blamer. She considers fellatio disgusting and sinful and unnatural, something that "normal, decent people" don't do. But her need was constant: "Some days without sex I felt I'd die." And always guilty: "Doctor, am I oversexed? As a sickness, I mean. Am I a nympho?"

Christine drifted into prostitution, but on a higher social level (call girl, rather than whore). She had strong suicidal tendencies, and underwent various melodramatic events. Through nonmoralistic and rather active-directed therapy, she was distinctly helped. Shiff ends with the words: "Nymphomania can be cured!"

The story of Christine, although it has an atypical racial angle, is a highly documented history of a self-blamer with an exceptionally low self-image, and as such may offer a clue to many other compulsively oversexed persons.

The hypererotic female was studied briefly in an authoritative work (Oliven, 1955) intended to be read almost exclusively by professional therapists. Oliven makes a distinction between three types of such conditons: (1) acute or sub-acute states of abnormal sexual (or pseudosexual) excitement; (2) chronic compulsive and impulsional promiscuity; (3) true obsessional "erotomanias." In the last-named group, Oliven describes a case in which the patient cannot get sex off her mind:

Everything seems to remind her of genital or sexual symbols; or she may not be able to read anything without searching for, or discovering, hidden obscene meanings; or she may endlessly doodle and draw sexual symbols. In a more severe form the patient may be convinced that a strange man, or even acquaintance, is in love with her; she may pursue him, perhaps accuse him, and eventually hallucinate that he visits her through a window at night.

Oliven is here dealing with persecution mania and paranoia, as linked to nymphomania, rather than the usual activities in which the sexual desire is conscious and recognized as such by the patient, and is acted out in the form of promiscuous sex behavior. He finds that most of the classic cases of nymphomania in the medical and medicolegal literature "were quite clearly early symptoms of a psychosis, probably mostly schizophrenia, perhaps some manic excitement states."

Louis London finds that "nymphomania is not rare," that it is usually found in women who do not attain an orgasm, although he reports a case (London, 1957a) in which one does indeed come to orgasm, and he comments that the reason that literature contains few case histories and almost nothing about the psychodynamics of this state is because "only a few of the women who have this deviation consult a physician."

In the one case outlined by London, the married girl is troubled by her inability to remain faithful. She goes with single and married men, searches for new men, picks them up everywhere. Each time she swears off men, and each time she goes back, remorseful and guilty. She performs fellatio, and likes to bite men on the neck and shoulders until she draws blood—this combination is termed *vampirism* by London. But her problem is largely one of self-image and lack of control: "She readily admits that she has indulged sexually with over one hundred men during the past three years. She says she is oversexed and cannot control her compulsion to go out with any man who accosts her." But at the same time she wants a husband, and a home "for my baby and security and happiness which I have never had."

One case (Karpman, 1954) is analyzed in classic Freudian terms. The patient, formerly a prostitute and now a secretary, came for treatment because of recurrences of absentmindedness at the typewriter—frequently typing two lines on the same space. Well educated and of respectable family, she had

86

drifted into a life of promiscuity in her early years as a manifestation "of aggression against her parents." During her teens, she left home, became a prostitute, then went to live with a wealthy farmer. When he tried to leave her to get married, she shot and killed him. After which:

She kept the clippings of the widely-publicized trial and showed them proudly. She became secretary to her lawyer who was also a dog breeder. She avoided intimate relations with men; her interest in sex petered out and she led a conservative and respectable life. The basic factor was father fixation and hate of the mother. Her first lover was a father image. Exhibitionism was satisfied by the publicity of the trial. Strong latent homosexuality was revealed; she was proud of the affair with the man she killed, a well-known Don Juan. A girl with a strong father fixation more frequently becomes a nymphomaniac or prostitute. Homosexual tendencies are shown in her hatred toward men, her psychosexual infantilism. Her lover fitted into the bisexual pattern. His betrayal brought about narcissistic injury, he became the target of violent hatred; he represented the whole male sex. Homicide discharged her hate and restored narcissism. The homosexual component was sublimated in dog breeding. The typewriter spacer represents an unconscious desire to relive dramatic experience, to alleviate intolerable guilt. She reproduced symbolically her last meeting with her lover but this time did not pull the spacer, i.e., refrained from pulling the trigger . . .

For many readers, this might appear a parody of Freudianism, but it does come from a serious researcher.

In another work consisting of detailed case histories of twenty-three individuals having abnormal sexual behavior patterns (London, 1957b), no hypererotic heterosexual woman is described, although there is an interesting study of a male counterpart to the nymphomaniac, a man afflicted with satyriasis. The oversexed male, in our society, is less likely to constitute a problem for himself than is the oversexed female, and the serious literature on the satyr is therefore seldom encountered.

It can be seen from the above summary of recent litera-

87

ture that genuine cases of nymphomania are seldom reported or analyzed, and that conjecture and prejudice are still found in abundance. Although there have been studies of individual cases, there have been no systematic collective studies from which generalized conclusions as to the causes of this phenomenon can be drawn, consistent with our knowledge of the physiology and psychology of woman.

10

Physiological Factors

IN THE EARLY PERIOD OF SEX RESEARCH, SOCIALLY condemned sexual behavior was generally attributed either to moral or to hereditary and congenital factors, and sometimes to a combination of both. People who indulged in homosexuality, promiscuity, prostitution and even masturbation were evil—they were assumed to lack will power and to have no moral or ethical standards. These acts were considered morally equivalent to robbery, murder, or cannibalism.

Yet, even while being condemned, the same people were in a sense exonerated, because the feeling persisted (Krafft-Ebing, 1922; Havelock Ellis, 1936) that the sexually disturbed were born that way. Exactly what there was in the anatomical and physiological setup that led to the deviant sex behavior was not understood. The condition was described, if not as hereditary, then at least as congenital. The term used in the literature to describe such a state was "constitutional."

Freud continued to adhere to the concept of constitutional predisposition to neurotic and psychotic behavior patterns. However, his main emphasis and that of almost all followers, neo-Freudians and non-Freudians, was on the early learned conditioning of a human being. This conditioning resulted in compulsive, deviated, or otherwise disturbed behavior. Theories of hereditary or congenital sexual disturbance are still articulated, particularly with regard to homosexuality. A summary of the research on this problem, made by one of the authors (Ellis, 1963f), demonstrates that there is little scientific evidence for such a contention. Such theories are probably held today, as one researcher (Cory, 1963) notes, primarily because of a vested interest in them, rather than because they are validated.

Nevertheless, nymphomania may not be in the same category as homosexuality, sadism, masochism and other forms of deviant sexual behavior. The possibility of physiological factors (genetic, or developing later in life) cannot be entirely discounted. For whereas in homosexuality we are dealing with the *direction* of the libidinal energy, with the nature of the sex object, in nymphomania we are dealing with the *power* of the sex drive, its insatiability, and the resurgence of interest to which it leads.

It is difficult to imagine the physiological factors that would account for a male being sexually frightened of females, or being aroused exclusively by other males, or for his delighting in whipping or being whipped. But it is not at all difficult to postulate psychological conditions, as did Freud, Adler, Horney and other psychotherapists, that may cause such deviations; now, analytic studies of numerous individuals present some evidence that their postulations may be valid.

On the other hand, while there is evidence that many cases of nymphomania have their origin in environmental conditions, (and it is possible that *all* cases must include *some* psychological causative conditions,) it is reasonable to believe that physiological disturbances of the brain, endocrine system or other parts of the body may also result in nymphomania. Physical anomalies may prevent orgasm in an otherwise highly-sexed woman, who hence remains unfulfilled and continues her ceaseless search; they may cause imbalance of sex hormones which leads to hypersexuality; or they may otherwise result in unusual psychophysical conditions which in turn foster nymphomania.

Menopause and nymphomania

Several suggestions of physiological causes of nymphomania have been made, but in none of these instances has the suggested anatomical anomaly *invariably* resulted in compulsive promiscuity. This would indicate that, although certain physiological changes may trigger off nymphomania, they only do so when *psychological predispositions* in this direction also exist.

One of the frequently recurring references to physiological causes of nymphomania concerns the menopause or female climacteric. As Kelly (1961) has pointed out, the entire question of "change of life" (an unfortunate phrase) is beset with legends, fears, apprehensions, and misapprehensions, all of which have probably done more harm that could be effected by any of the physical changes that do occur.

According to Kelly, the libido (of the average, nonpathological woman) "will not undergo any change just because she is passing through the change—at least not for quite some time, or even then." Under certain circumstances, dyspareunia, or painful intercourse, occurs as a result of alterations in the estrogen development—but this would result in less sexual desire, not more.

One researcher (Oliven, 1955) similarly asserts that "no major change is detectable (in the majority of cases) in the libido of a wife who passes through the menopause." However, he cites some instances where there is an abrupt increase, a frantic desire, to "grasp it before it is too late," a freedom from fear of impregnation—but these are all psychological conditions resulting from the woman's view of her physical state, rather than from the physical state itself.

Pruritus vulvae, or an itching of the vulva and the closely related area, sometimes accompanies menopause, and is probably due to the endocrinological changes that are taking place. Oliven points out that this itching "may lead a naïve woman to seek relief in increased relations; however, this activity is often short-lived as the friction, together with scratching, may irritate the vulva, produce tenderness, and at times cause secondary infection." Oliven then proceeds to point out that the "so-called 'acute idiopathic nymphomania' of some involuting women is most probably a symptom of an intense but covert anxiety state or similar psychic syndrome."

It would seem, then, from this and other studies of the climacteric, that where (in the relatively few instances) the increase in sex desire reaches a point beyond control, there are accompanying psychogenic factors that account for this development. It is more likely that men and women who have been somewhat inhibited in their sex relations, particularly by fear of the woman's pregnancy and their mutual dislike of contraceptive techniques, may find themselves able to enjoy a fuller and better sex life after a wife passes her menopause. In such cases, there may appear to be an increase in the wife's desire, but her activities tend to be normal, well-controlled, nonpathological—and cannot be identified with nymphomania.

Several other causes of hypersexuality in the female have been suggested from time to time. These include hyperthyroidism—particularly, according to Oliven, in the early stages of this pathological condition.

Numerous authors have mentioned nymphomania as manifest during moderately advanced stages of *pulmonary tuberculosis,* and this in turn has been attributed by some to the chronic low-grade fever. But most women suffering from this type of tubercular ailment do not develop strong, almost

91

uncontrollable sex interests. Where they do, it would appear that the psychological factors accompanying their physical condition (that is, depressed mental attitude, search for escape or relief, and proximity to males in a similar situation) rather than the physical condition per se, are primary determinants.

Brain damage of various types has been reported as resulting in nymphomania, but in almost all instances mentioned, hypersexuality did not always follow a particular kind of injury. In a few cases, the brain damage alone, quite unaccompanied by any environmental preconditioning, seems to have resulted in feminine hypersexuality. Thus, Oliven summarizes several circumstances in which increased libido has been observed *at times* in the female: "Following encephalitis or head injury (apparently involving the anterior pituitary); possibly in some cases of post-encephalitic Parkinsonism; and very acutely in an occasional medically uncontrolled epileptic female before, after, perhaps instead of, a seizure."

There has been considerable speculation with regard to the relationship between libidinal energy and *sex hormones*. Many laymen have assumed that undersexed people are deficient in hormones, and the oversexed are suffering from an abundance of such hormones. Ironically enough, it is not a plethora of the female sex hormones (or estrogens), but of the male hormones, or androgens, that may result in an increase in sex desire in the woman (Kupperman, 1961).

It is important here to emphasize that the terms "female sex hormones" and "male sex hormones" do not refer to chemical bodies or secretions that have a sex object as the target, but are "female" or "male" in the sense that they result in the development of secondary sexual characteristics (i.e., the development of the bust in the woman, of hair on the face in the man).

Kupperman describes the mechanism by which the androgens, and not the estrogens, account for the enhanced sexual drive in the woman:

> The logic for the use of this steroid [androgens] becomes apparent if we accept the premise that the center of eroticism in the female lies in the area of the clitoris. Since this organ with its rich nerve supply represents the phallic anlage in the female, its response to androgens would be anticipated. Evidence from many clinical reports and observations has established unequivocally the role of androgens in enhancing libido in the female.

92

When massive doses of androgens are used for therapeutic purposes, particularly in cases of cancer, greatly increased libido sometimes accompanies such therapy. However, in such instances, the debilitated physical condition, the fears of the patient, and the focusing on the deterioration and nonfunctioning of the body, often counteract the effects of the androgens as a sexually-increasing force. An endocrine imbalance, in which the androgens are present in the female body far beyond the normal needs, results in the syndrome known as virilism (Allen *et al.*, 1938) which in turn may be accompanied by high, uncontrolled sex interests. In this case, the nymphomania and the virilism are concomitant results of one factor: androgen content.

Adrenalectomy is mentioned as a possible cause of nymphomania (Allen, 1949). Actually, there are two adrenal glands, the medulla and the cortex, and it is not clear as to the nature of the operation that took place in the case described by Allen. Apparently it was the cortex that was removed. Only in recent years, since the development of cortisone and ACTH, has it been possible to remove the adrenal glands and have patients continue to live, and there is still a poverty of reports on the sex lives of these patients after surgery. It would seem that we are here confronted with a special aspect of hormonal imbalance, closely related to the problem of the androgens.

The most frequent *physiological* cause of nymphomania that appears in the literature is *the inability* (for physical rather than psychological reasons) of the woman *to achieve orgasm*. Such women, if they do not become frigid, may become insatiable. However, the inability to achieve orgasm is not necessarily physiological in origin; it may be due entirely to psychic blocks. When there are physiological difficulties, these are often traced to androgen deficiencies, thus leading to the paradoxical but logical conclusion that nymphomania may in some instances be caused by an overabundance of androgens, in other instances by a deficiency of these androgens.

Finally, a clue to the physiological causes of nymphomania (particularly those traced to brain injury, as mentioned earlier) may be found in work now being done (Delgado, 1963) with what has come to be known as ESB or electrical stimulation of the brain. As described by Delgado:

Under the influence of electrical stimulation of the brain

the cats and monkeys performed like electrical toys. Depending on which "button" was pressed by the investigators, one of a great variety of motor responses was evoked ... In some cases ... the "will" of the animal apparently opposed the response evoked by the mild electrical excitation, and the movement would not be made. However, when stronger stimulations were applied this opposition broke down and the animal responded as "directed."

The effects of the stimulation were many: they included fits of rage, aggression, destruction and friendliness. In the course of these studies, it was found that the part of the brain that had to be stimulated to bring on such rage was the amygdala. Now, acute hypersexuality in the female or the male seems to result when the amygdala is physically damaged, malfunctioning or in disharmony with other parts of the brain and the body. In such instances, it is hardly likely that psychotherapy could prove effective in reducing the sexual tension. We may even have here a rare physiological condition that, although not necessary, is sufficient to produce nymphomania.

In general, the etiology of nymphomania must usually be sought in a woman's psychological attitudes, rather than her peculiar physiology. People have commented that many "nymphomaniacs" are fat, but obesity can hardly be said to be a sufficient cause. We may surmise, instead, that many fat women in our society see themselves as so undesirable that they find it necessary to be in a constant state of sexiness to feel wanted, or that many women are so emotionally disturbed that they bring on the concomitant neurotic symptoms of (a) being seriously overweight, and (b) being compulsively promiscuous.

Man is both a rational and an irrational animal; he is often self-destructive in choosing a path of short-range rather than long-range hedonism; he overgeneralizes, indulges in self-pity, creates myths that are self-defeating, and (particularly in the field of sex) builds unnecessary taboos, cages, and restrictions.

In our society, and with our biological heritage, men and women can very easily become disturbed sexually, and it is entirely *possible* that some people, certainly many of the psychotics, are born with physical, chemical, and endocrine conditions that predispose them to becoming more disturbed than the average person. It is possible, or even probable, that such individuals, given psychological conditions favorable to the development of a sexual deviation, would be more likely to respond in a neurotic manner than would others. Such people may, in certain instances, be predisposed to be obsessive-compulsive or psychotic; and with the proper physiological and/or environment factors, they might develop into nymphomaniacs. This is not to say, however, that compulsive promiscuity usually, or even frequently, is directly or primarily caused by physiological aberrations (except, as noted, for that rare condition, *true* nymphomania). *The major cause of disturbed hypersexuality in women is psychological, environmental, and social;* and the major area of treatment must be psychotherapeutic.

To summarize: If we wish to distinguish among the varieties of nymphomania, then it is probably safe to say that the vast majority of, and perhaps all, *true or endogenous nymphomaniacs* are physiologically driven women who have practically no control over their sex urges, and who are literally impelled by brain lesions, hormonal imbalances, or other physical anomalies to run from one man to another. These woman are rare.

A second class consists of *manic nymphomaniacs*, outrightly psychotic women, some of them in temporary hypomanic states and some of them permanently deranged, who also find it impossible to control themselves in their search for sexual appeasement. These manic nymphomaniacs also, in all probability, have some underlying physiological anomaly, neurological or hormonal, which predisposes them to be psychotic; their psychosis, in turn, drives them to compulsive promiscuity. In their case, however, psychological or environmental influences also significantly contribute to their emotional aberrations, and thus indirectly are important causative factors in their nymphomania.

A third class of nymphomaniac includes *physically hypersexed* females such as those afflicted with virilism, who have exceptionally strong innate sex drives, and who *could* theoretically control their urges, but who do not do so to any great extent. These highly-sexed women find it most difficult, but not *impossible*, to follow the sex mores of our restrictive society. Some, therefore, undisciplinedly give in to their strong sex urges and become nymphomaniacs; while most of them manage to live adequately, if somewhat uncomfortably, with their powerful libido—an adjustment by which they have sex relations in a somewhat promiscuous but hardly compulsive or disordered manner.

A fourth class of nymphomaniacs consists of women who have quite normal physical sex drives, but who for various *psychological* reasons, compulsively drive themselves to have indiscriminate relations with males. The majority of nymphomaniacs, including most of those described in this book, would appear to be in this class.

A fifth class consists of women who are relatively low-sexed physiologically, and who have some difficulty in achieving orgasm even though they are capable of some degree of sexual arousal. These women, like those in the fourth class, may also for various psychological reasons, including their dissatisfaction with their sexual functioning, drive themselves into indiscriminate serial or simultaneous sex affairs with many men.

There would almost seem to be a continuum of nymphomaniacs, ranging from those whose sexual compulsivity is almost entirely caused by the anomalous physiological urges, to those whose compulsive indiscriminateness is entirely of psychological origin. However, those who are driven to their disordered sexual activity by psychological factors may have some kind of underlying physiological abnormality which partly or largely causes their psychological disturbances.

So, directly or indirectly, physical factors in nymphomania are not to be minimized. *Nonetheless, we again must point out that in the great majority of cases of compulsive promiscuity, psychological issues are of prime importance, and any physical therapy that may be instituted should be accompanied by intensive psychotherapy.*

Of all of these types of oversexuality, the one that has attracted the greatest attention, and that seems to combine physiological and psychological factors, is the inability of the woman to achieve an orgasm. Some have even defined nymphomania exclusively by this characteristic, and many have contended that this is *the* outstanding reason why women run from one bed to another, to find gratification.

Actually, it is not true, in our experience, that many women who cannot reach orgasm become nymphomaniacs, or that most compulsively promiscuous women find it impossible to have an orgasm. Both contentions seem to be exaggerations and overgeneralizations. Many who cannot obtain the orgasm do go frantically from man to man. Others, frustrated and unsatisfied, turn to masturbation or to lesbianism, or they simply become frigid. They may in some instances consider themselves hopeless, and stop trying; or they may consider all males hopeless—and withdraw from the heterosexual field.

As a matter of fact, most compulsively oversexed women (but not all) do achieve orgasm, and—even more than other women—they tend to achieve it during penile-vaginal intercourse.

When one turns to those women who rarely or never have an orgasm, it is doubtful that this is the true cause of the nymphomania. Such a woman is either unable to obtain an orgasm under any circumstances, or she is able to do so, but has not yet brought it about. If she is in the first group, then she has not yet come to the realization that promiscuity will not answer her problems. And, if in the second group, she can be shown that it would be much more sensible for her to remain with one male who cares for her than to try the field. Such a woman may be upset, not only by the failure to obtain orgasm and the consequent lack of relief from tension but also, and more important, because she considers herself worthless for not having obtained it.

Thus are physiological and psychological factors intertwined. Many women who years ago would not have been concerned if they didn't achieve orgasm and who would have been happy with the nonorgasmic pleasures of sex, or who might even have been content to have little or no sexual satisfaction, today believe that if they fail to achieve sexual climax they are inadequate and worthless. And just as they try hard to gain a husband, or to raise children who are better than other people's children, or to have a fine career, they now try to achieve mightily in terms of orgasm.

It is not the lack of orgasm which bothers these women, it is the lack of *achievement*. They are afraid of failure, and they see themselves as absolutely no good. They, usually, are taking the perfectly logical thought, "I do not like the fact of not achieving orgasm and not getting pleasure thereby," which *normally* leads to the idea, "Now let's see what I can do about this fact that I do not like." But they *then* irrationally go on to a different thought, "Because I do not like this fact, I can't stand it." Or: "Because I am not achieving the satisfaction which I theoretically could obtain in intercourse,

97

I am worthless." And it is this second, insane, thought which upsets them, not the fact that they fail to obtain orgasms.

Let us put this differently, in terms of the A-B-C theory of personality (Ellis, 1962a; Ellis and Harper, 1961a, 1961b) that explains many of the aberrations of human personality. In the usual case, the individual who gets overexcited, upset or neurotic at point C, erroneously tends to believe that it is something that happened at point A which made her excited or upset or neurotic. Thus, she usually says: "At point A I did not get what I want, and therefore I became upset at point C." In seeing things in this manner, however, she is quite mistaken because it is not her frustration at point A which causes her neurotic or disturbed reaction (at point C). It is B, or what she tells herself about the disappointment or frustration at point A.

In other words, no matter what happens to an individual at point A, aside from her receiving actual physical injury and pain, the reason she gets upset at point C is because she obviously is telling herself at point B, "I can't stand this happening at point A! It is terrible, it is awful, it is catastrophic; it makes me an utterly worthless individual." If, on the other hand, she said at point B, "I *can* stand this unfortunate event, such as sexual frustration, which has occurred at point A. I'll never like it, but I can stand it," then, at point C, she would experience relatively mild emotions of disappointment, sorrow, regret, annoyance or frustration—but she would not get the violent negative emotions of anxiety, depression, anger, hostility, and grandiosity.

In the case of the lack of orgasm on the part of the woman (which, let us assume, is happening at Point A), if she were telling herself sanely at point B: "I am not getting the orgasm that I theoretically could get—I dislike this, I regret that I am not getting it, I'm saddened by this loss—now let me see what I can do about this dislikable fact," she would *not* get terribly upset at any time at point C. Most frequently, in fact, she would be able to do something about what was happening at point A. That is to say, she would be able to go over her reaction, review what she and her partner did sexually, and change some of what he did or what she did, and ultimately she would achieve orgasm.

Even if she never achieved it (because, let us say, she had a kind of psychophysical makeup that was unorgasmic), she would still be able to tell herself at point B, "All right, I seem to be incapable of ever achieving an orgasm. That is sad, that is deplorable—but I can stand it. I can take it; it is not catastrophic; there are other pleasures in life, including sexual pleasures, which I can get, despite the fact that I'll never get orgasm." Once again, she would never be upset or neurotic at point C, even if she were not experiencing orgasm at point A.

Now, disturbed individuals (and, unfortunately, innumerable people in our society are emotionally disturbed) frequently do not think this *sane* way when they do not achieve orgasm. As noted before, the female who is not able to come to climax, especially who is not able to do so in penile-vaginal intercourse (which she wrongly construes as the only right and proper way to get it), often tells herself, "This is terrible, this is awful! I am not able to reach a climax and I may never be able to reach one, and this proves that there is something basically wrong with me as a person!" Consequently, she gets frantic and upset at point C.

Brain lesions, hormonal imbalance, adrenalectomy, and other physiological conditions may indeed result in nymphomania. But the major physical condition, namely the inability to achieve orgasm, may in most instances be psychologically induced. It would seem to be a result, rather than a cause. And even where the inability to achieve orgasm is causative, the main area of disturbance that led to nymphomania would seem to be *the attitude toward the failure,* rather than the failure itself.

11

Parental Conditioning

EARLY—AND LATER—RESEARCH THREW LITTLE LIGHT on the origins of nymphomania, one reason being the limitations imposed by the emphasis on anatomical and physiological considerations. To explain the development of a deviant pattern such as nymphomania, one is compelled to turn to the complex interaction of environmental factors: cultural and personal, social and psychological.

According to the orthodox Freudians and to the orthodox behaviorists, parental conditioning, especially in the first few years of life, is at the bottom of practically all psychological disturbance. Devotees of these two schools of thought believe that human beings are born plastic, that they do not have any pre-set ideas and, consequently, what they learn in their early impressionable years stays with them. If this early learning is of a warped and hyperemotional nature, it is presumed the children become warped and hyperemotional.

The Freudians, in particular, believe that if an individual undergoes severe oedipal conflict during early childhood (i.e., he lusts after his mother, his father becomes jealous, and he feels guilty) the effects of this oedipal complex will remain with him throughout his life, unless he overcomes them through intensive psychoanalysis. Similarly, in the female, the Freudians believe that what happens to a young girl in her early childhood, sometimes in the first two years of life, is so crucial that it can affect her for the rest of her days. Consequently, if a girl is a nymphomaniac, then, *according to this theory,* she was made so by early parental conditioning.

A great deal of evidence has accumulated in recent years that throws much doubt on this Freudian concept. Although it is quite true that all of us are enormously influenced by early childhood, it also seems to be true that *the inborn genetic tendencies which we have at birth make us differen-*

100

tially conditionable. That is to say, a child who may be born with a hyperactive nervous system will tend to be highly conditioned in a certain direction if acted on by her parents while she is quite young. But *another child* with a *different kind of nervous system* will *not* be so strongly conditioned.

Moreover, there is a reciprocal action in the conditioning of children. A child, for example, who is born with a tendency to be high-strung, nasty, or difficult during her first few years, will put such a strain on her parents that they, in turn, will act differently toward her than they would toward another of their children who behaves in a more agreeable manner. Consequently it is not merely the conditions that the parents impose on the child that influence her behavior and character, but to a certain degree it is the conditions *that the child imposes on the parents,* and through which she thereby influences the parents to apply certain conditions to herself.

A lot of the conditioning that does take place occurs during *later* childhood. Adolescents in our society tend to be conformist and to do most things that their peer group asks them to do. This kind of conformity, drilled into the child during adolescence, may affect her more significantly than some of the things she learned (and forgot) during earlier training.

What is more, there is reason to believe the powers of the sex drives are inborn, although the way in which we manifest these drives is largely the result of conditioning. Some of us are born with highly active sexual drives, while others are born with less active sexual drives; these two types of individuals will be differently conditioned. It is observable that children in the same family who are given exactly the same kind of restrictive upbringing may not react to it in the same way. One of them may really be suppressed (and repressed all her life) while the other one blithely engages in overt sex relations at an early age, and, while she feels guilty about doing so, she continues. The one who rebels may have an innately stronger sex drive.

Is one justified in concluding, as the Freudians and behaviorists tend to do, that nymphomania is acquired as the result of early parental conditioning? There are certainly some nymphomaniacs who seem to be born with a physiological, temperamental predisposition, to act in a certain manner. Even though these women might not necessarily grow up to be nymphomaniacs, their inborn tendencies make it easier for them to do so.

Nevertheless, there *are* important aspects of parental con-

101

ditioning which motivate some females to become overly promiscuous. For example, some girls are so thoroughly held down by their parents, in sexual and non-sexual ways, that they look forward all through their adolescence to getting away from parental discipline, and perhaps to doing things that would spite their parents. Raised in an ultra-restrictive fashion, and rebelling against this, once they get away from the home they may go to the opposite extreme and bed with every boy they meet to show that they are not going to kowtow to parental authority any longer.

On the other side of the fence, there are girls raised in a liberal atmosphere by parents who may literally encourage promiscuity. And a few of these girls become promiscuous not because they really wish to do so, or are so impelled by their own sex drives, but because in their subculture they would be nonconformists if they did not; and rather than be nonconformists, they become conformingly promiscuous.

There are still other girls who are raised to hate themselves. Continually criticized by their parents, they come to hate and criticize themselves; later—they try to be loved by everybody else. Consequently, as we have shown in cases already discussed, these girls may become compulsively promiscuous. They are conditioned in a way which is not necessarily directly sexual, but which causes them to have low self-esteem. As we have indicated, it is more likely to be a girl's *ideas about herself* and her personal worth which drive her to sexual promiscuity than her specific ideas about sex.

RUTH X.

Ruth's family was European. They strongly believed the man was the center of the household, and that the woman should be subservient. Consequently, her mother and father favored her two brothers, and generally acted as if she were worthless because she was a female—while her brothers were revered. The family was not particularly restrictive—her father had a mistress for a good deal of his married life, and his wife knew this and accepted it. The sons were encouraged by their father and the mother to have sex relations with prostitutes and young girls, to their heart's content.

Ruth was taught that, as a girl, she was not allowed the freedom of the boys; but no special rules were laid down against her having sexual affairs. So she was not rebelling against sexual rigidity when she began, at the age of eighteen, to be promiscuous with boys. The thing she was really rebelling against was that she, as a girl, was not supposed to do things the way she wanted to do them. She was supposed to check with her parents regarding her boyfriends, to marry the kind of boy that they would approve, and to refrain from having any ideas of her own. In rebellion against this, when she was in her first year of college she joined a radical organization of which her parents thoroughly disapproved, and started to participate in many activities which would be anathema to them. Not that they would be specifically against her having sexual affairs; they were against her doing almost anything on her own, without their consent—and sex was included in this.

Moreover, Ruth found, or thought she found, that by having sex relations with boys, she could reduce and control them. She was a good-looking girl, attractive to a great many boys. At first she used the plan of disdaining males, trying to hurt them by her rejections. Then she found an even better tactic. She accepted males, quickly had sex relations, and then showed them she did not love them, was not in the least dependent on them, and was not willing to do the things they wanted. This, she believed, would reduce the male to his proper place. Thus she reacted directly against her early upbringing.

With a new-found feeling of independence, Ruth felt she was getting along quite well in her rebellion. When her parents complained about her staying out late at night, or about some other real or suspected activities, she simply told them to go to hell. Even when they deprived her of support, she found she could obtain a few dollars from male friends. Not that she had sex on a prostitutional basis; she told the men what was happening with her parents, and they obliged with small sums of money.

Ruth tried to be happy in her rebellion and independence. She was having a variety of sex relations which her parents could not help knowing about, especially *since she could not be content as a rebel unless there was some awareness on their part*. However, there was the annoying (and significant) matter of three pregnancies, the consequent abortions, and all the anguish, fears, furtive plans, despondency and self-degradation that accompany such operations in the American society.

Where was it all leading? Was sex pleasurable when it went beyond control? Ruth had herself fitted for a diaphragm, but could not bring herself to use it regularly, complaining that it interfered with her pleasure. Later, it became clear she was revolting against "rules" (such as using a diaphragm), just as she had revolted against her parents. But she discriminated poorly between instances when rebellion aided her, as to some degree it did with her parents, and when it defeated her own ends.

There followed difficulties with school authorities: violation of curfew, apprehension of a man in her dormitory room. The school complained to the parents who were distressed but felt unable to exercise further control over their daughter. Finally there came suspension from classes and a warning that the next infraction would bring expulsion.

Serious about the pursuit of a career, and fearing that expulsion would prevent admission to another school, Ruth became despondent and disturbed. At last, she came for psychotherapy.

The emptiness of her life with boys had become increasingly apparent. The attachments, Ruth knew, were neither deep nor satisfying. She avoided longterm involvements, found every man wanting in one respect or another, and feared that marriage would lead to domination by her husband, just as her early life had been dominated by her parents.

Yet, her girlfriends were doing very well with boys, and were marrying, while she was getting nowhere. Ruth wanted her career, but she also looked forward to a monogamous relationship, and to children. While she enjoyed some aspects of her promiscuity, other factors were negative.

In the sex act, Ruth generally had a pleasant time. Precisely because she had a variety of partners, she had no difficulties in the act.

Ruth's was a clear-cut instance of parental conditioning. Let us look at what happens to a girl like this in therapy. (We will return later to a more generalized discussion of the treatment of nymphomaniacs.)

In Ruth's case, I employed the general principles of rational-emotive psychotherapy (Ellis, 1957, 1962a, 1962b, 1964). This consisted of showing her that—as with many rebels—she was cutting off her nose to spite her face. Rather than having become independent of her parents, *Ruth had strengthened her dependency.* When I first brought this to her attention, she was shocked—and skeptical. But I showed her, in an early session, that anybody who rebels violently and angrily against someone else, obviously is ruled by some of the ideas of this other person. Otherwise, she would *quietly* disagree with these ideas. The fact that Ruth protested *so much* against parental authority, meant that she was still influenced by that

104

authority. True, this was a negative influence. But she was being censored by her parents' attitude and behavior. She was *not* developing an independent existence as, in her delusions, she had supposed.

Against this, Ruth argued vehemently, insisting she was doing what she wanted to do, rather than what her parents wanted her to do. But I showed her this was a logical error, because to do what she wanted to do herself would normally have little or no relationship to what someone else wanted her to do. If, for example, she enjoyed hiking and engineering, and had taken up these pursuits only because she enjoyed them, there would be a good chance that her parents would have little feeling about these same things. But if it so happened her parents thought it horrible for her to enjoy hiking and engineering and then, oddly enough, she did enjoy precisely those, and only those, avocations, her enjoyment would probably be related to her enjoying their disenjoyment—and would indicate that she was negatively ruled by their rules.

This was what Ruth finally had to admit—because, oddly enough, almost all the things she enjoyed in life happened to be activities to which her parents were strongly opposed. This (to me, and to Ruth after I pointed it out to her) was highly suspicious!

In addition, those things which her parents would have liked Ruth to do, such as marry and have children, which she said she wanted to do, were events with which she was getting nowhere. So, even in situations where it looked as if Ruth was going along with her parents, things were not working out. She was, obviously, successful only when opposing their wishes.

After we had gone through many examples, Ruth was willing to admit she did many things mainly because her parents were on the opposite side of the fence. Combatting her parents' desires was probably her prime motive in living and acting. So, in a true sense, the parents and their views still controlled Ruth's behavior.

I particularly worked with Ruth on her *anger* against her parents, and tried to show her that anger, hostility or over-rebellion against anybody, including parents, is invariably unwise *because it defeats one's own ends*. Not that it isn't human for all of us to become angry when we are frustrated, particularly when our parents are negative as Ruth's were to her. It is very easy; but the fact that it's easy doesn't mean that it's good. Even though anger is normal (we are biologically as well as sociologically inclined to feel it on many

105

occasions), this does not mean that we should cherish our anger—any more than the fact that it is normal to acquire a cold means we have to do nothing about warding one off.

At first, I had a great deal of difficulty with Ruth because she thought, as most people think, that she had very good reasons to be hostile to her parents. "Look," she said, "haven't I given you enough evidence that they are against me, that they won't give me the leeway a girl my age should have?"

"Yes," I replied, "you've given me that evidence, and I agree that your parents are restricting you more than is reasonable."

"Well, then, isn't it right for me to be angry at them?"

"No, you're confusing two things. It's right, meaning correct, for you to be irritated by them, but anger is not the same as irritation and annoyance."

"What do you mean by that?"

"Well, try to define the elements of frustration and annoyance—and, of anger. Let's take frustration first. Frustration means you're not getting what you want. That's exactly what you tell yourself: 'I'm not getting what I want, and I don't like it.' Isn't that what frustration means?"

"Yes, it certainly does. But isn't that exactly my situation...I'm not getting what I want, and I don't like what I'm getting?"

"Yes, that is exactly your situation. But that's *it! Stop*, right there."

"Do you mean that I should just accept the fact I'm not getting what I want even though I don't like it?"

"Yes, unless there's a possibility of change. If you could change your parents, and get them to give you more independence, by all means do so. But is there any such possibility?"

"No, there damn well isn't."

"All right, then. Let's assume that, as long as you're living at home and are supported by them—as you have to be until you get through school—they are going to be the way they are, and they will continue to frustrate you."

"Yes, I guess that's a safe assumption," Ruth said. "They've done it for years and I see no reason why they won't continue."

"Fine," I noted. "So let's assume they're going to continue to frustrate you. Now, if you were just saying, 'I have been frustrated by them, that's too bad,' then you'd feel what?"

"I'd feel frustrated."

"Yes, that's exactly what you'd feel: annoyed, irritated,
106

frustrated; you'd feel sad that they're frustrating you in such a manner, and you're not getting what you want. Now, let's go on a bit to the anger."

"But isn't it the same thing? Because I feel frustrated, don't I then get angry?"

"No, of course not. In order to feel angry you have to add a perfectly idiotic sentence to your first sentence."

"What's this idiotic sentence?"

"It's: 'Because I am frustrated, and I don't like being frustrated, I *shouldn't* be.' Or, putting it the way we usually say to ourselves: 'They *shouldn't* frustrate me the way they do.' "

"But *should* they?"

"No, not in the sense you mean, in the sense you are now asking the question. What you mean, 'Is it nice of them to frustrate me? Are they doing the right thing to me, their daughter?' In that sense, no, they *should not,* it would be nicer if they didn't frustrate you. But you're not using the word *should* in just that way."

"Well how else am I using it?"

"You're using it in an absolutistic sense. When you say they should not frustrate you, don't you really mean the world should be arranged in such a manner that your parents are *not allowed* to frustrate you?"

"But should the world be arranged so that my parents *are* allowed to frustrate me?"

"Well, why shouldn't it?"

Ruth stopped for a moment to think and then said, "I just don't quite see it yet."

"All right," I persisted, "let's go over it again. The world *is* the way it is. You *do* have parents who frustrate you, and we agree it would be better if they didn't. But they *are* frustrating you. Now, why should the world be different, so that you have different parents, or you have the same parents— —who suddenly, magically, become nonfrustrating?"

"Well, why shouldn't it be better?"

"You mean that you would *like* it to be better, don't you?"

"Yes, that's what I mean."

"And what you *really* mean is that because you would like the world to be better, would like fate to be kind, like things to be better for you—therefore the world and your parents *should* be better. Now, is that a sensible statement—just because you would like the world to change, it *should* change?"

Again, Ruth thought for awhile. She said, "No, I guess there *is* something wrong with that."

107

"Well, think about it some more," I said. "And the more you think about it, the more you'll see there is something radically wrong. Not, again, that it wouldn't be lovely and fair for your parents to behave differently and the world to be better. It *would* be lovely and fair."

I worked with Ruth some more on this, and finally, she saw there is never any reason why something *should* be, just because we would like it to be, and it would be fairer if it were so. For there *is* no thoroughgoing justice in the world; and the world and the people in it *are* frequently unfair and unjust, overdemanding and too authoritative. It would be lovely if it were not so; but it is so, and we give ourselves entirely gratuitous pain when we refuse to accept its being so.

As I said to Ruth, "It certainly would be silly if I expected you to like your parents' being the way they are, because we are assuming they are dislikable, and not only dislikable as far as you're concerned, but probably to most others who might have them as parents. I'm not trying to get you to like the way they are, I'm trying to get you to suffer it *gracefully*."

Then she said again, almost angrily, "Why *should* I accept the way they are?"

"Because it *would* aid you. This way you only give yourself more discomfort than they are giving you. While they're frustrating you, you're enormously frustrating *yourself* about being frustrated. You're saying, 'I can't stand to be frustrated, it's terrible being frustrated!' which aggravates the frustration. So, the reason you should gracefully accept them and their frustration is to help you live successfully in a world where things are not fair, not the way you would like them to be."

Again she thought awhile, then said, "Well, I guess you're telling me that it is possible for me to be happy, even in a world like the one I actually live in, where things are not going my way."

"Yes, that's exactly what I *am* telling you. Not that it's great to live in such a situation, and not that you should look forward to remaining in it. Naturally, since you're getting to the age where you'll be graduating from school and on your own, you should look forward to a different world—a world *you'll* create, a world in which you will live and work independently, or else live with a man and a family of your own choosing. That will be pleasant, that's what you should look forward to. But right now you can't do anything but look forward. In the *present* moment, you've just got to accept the way the world is, your world with your parents,

108

your school, and all your other existing problems. Or else!"

"By 'or else' you mean or else give myself a greater banging up than they're giving me?"

"Yes, exactly that."

Such conversation finally made a strong impression on Ruth. I find that in rational-emotive therapy this frequently happens. Patients talk things over with me, and I am able to show them how twisted is their thinking, and that this twisted thinking is the thing that upsets them, rather than the persons or the events impinging on them. They see this and feel better about it—but that doesn't mean they've really changed. Several days later they often slip back into the old ways of thinking, and upset themselves once again.

This is precisely what Ruth did, not once but many times, in the next few months. Each time I showed her she was defeating herself by not accepting reality, not facing the fact her parents were the way they were, she felt good; a few days later she would tend to slip back. When her mother and father did something of a restricting nature, or made a nasty remark, she would start getting angry all over again. And almost every time the same thing occurred: as soon as she was angry, almost the first thing she thought of was going to bed with a boy.

This was like alcohol to her; it made her feel better. The revenge she was getting on her parents was a delicious nectar and diverted her mind, at least temporarily, from any severe frustrations which they or anybody else imposed upon her.

Thus, Ruth would keep slipping back. Then, quietly, at her next session, I would go over with her again exactly what had happened, and show her she didn't go to bed with this boy because she enjoyed it; but once again she was controlled by the negative attitudes of her parents—and was still not doing anything constructive about her life.

Finally, after a number of months, Ruth became less and less excited about the things her parents were doing, although their behavior continued to be much the way it had been before.

The less disturbed she was, the less compulsive she would be about running off to have a sex affair. Once in a while she would do so for *other* reasons, but this I considered reasonably healthy. In this way, she might meet a good marital prospect; and rather than go through a slowpaced term of courtship, she decided she might better know a little more about such a man as soon as possible, and that the best place to learn what a human being thinks and feels is, often, in the bedroom.

Ruth would go to bed with these men quite quickly. Usually, she'd find they didn't have the depth of character she thought they had, and her infatuation would quickly fade. Philosophically she accepted the fact that each of these affairs was another learning experience. Not only did Ruth learn something about herself, but she also gained the valuable information that a particular man was not for her on a longterm basis.

Every so often, then, Ruth would be sexually unconventional for *good* reasons, but most often she would be promiscuous for *rebellious* reasons, because she was going to "fix her parents' wagon."

Finally, however, Ruth's rebellion disappeared and her affairs dwindled. By the time she left therapy, she was having one affair at a time, and it would usually last a few weeks or more. If she had no thought of marrying her lover, they would part, either at her instigation or at his, and she would start another affair.

Despite her parents' continual disapproval, Ruth kept calmly, this time really calmly, going about her own pattern of behavior, and doing it because she wanted to do it that way. When she finally left therapy she was following this pattern; and I later discovered that she had married and seemed to be doing well in her marriage.

JANE T.

In the case of Jane T., a twenty-one-year-old call girl I saw, the parental conditioning was almost the opposite of what occurred in Ruth's case. Jane's family wanted her to be an independent girl who stood on her own two feet, and who would excel in intellectual and scholastic affairs. Her father had not succeeded in life, but he had had a good education, including a university degree; her mother was a club woman with intellectual pretensions. Both parents kept after Jane, an only child, to read more and to know more than other children did, to be, perhaps, a scientist and far above ordinary people in her intellectual achievements.

Jane, who probably had a somewhat higher-than-average I.Q., was really not a bright girl. She soon discovered she just wasn't able to measure up to the aspirations of her parents. At first, she tried as hard as she could, but then she tended to give up and move into other fields. She was a warm and pleasant girl, and had many girlfriends. Then, as she went into high school, she found she had something else with which to gain attention, and that was blond hair, blue eyes, and a good body. She became very popular with the boys.

But the boys Jane went with, all carefully screened by her parents, were usually brighter and from a better social class than she. They found her lacking. Soon they became bored. If she wanted to hold them, she discovered, she would have to go to bed with them. This she promptly did.

Jane got into serious difficulties and was almost thrown out of high school, but she did get through. Then, after she went to work, her parents, extremely disappointed that she had not gone to college, insisted she not take an ordinary typing-secretarial job. Because they pushed her to work for which she was ill-equipped, Jane failed miserably in her first three jobs. Finally, she left home and came to New York City. She then sent a series of letters to her parents, telling them how well she was doing on a job which she didn't actually have (but which one of her girlfriends did have).

Actually, she began a life of prostitution. She enjoyed the prostitution to some degree, but she found little sexual pleasure in it. Her customers tended to be businessmen for whom she didn't care. But she did enjoy her ability to make a great deal of money with relatively little work, and to do some of the things which she had always wanted to—particularly, to spend money on clothes, cars, and other things.

Jane lived in fear that, one day her parents would come to the city and discover exactly what she was doing; but she managed to avoid that by frequently taking trips home. She saw them often enough so that they did not feel they had to check on her.

In any event, Jane didn't object to the life she was leading and did capitalize, to some degree, on her sexual activities. But she began to get into emotional trouble. She would find a customer she really liked, then stop charging him money (to which her syndicate objected), and to have sex relations with him on the basis of giving her body for his time. In other words, she repeated the same pattern she had followed in her high school days.

Jane became depressed when she could not win for herself one of the men she liked. She had a succession of lovers. Some treated her badly, some were reasonably nice, but she always aspired to a male definitely above her intellectual level. When she did go with such a man, she became so frightened he would leave her that she behaved more awkwardly than she normally did, under less threatening circumstances. Jane was almost tongue-tied with these men, never her normal, ebullient self. The more this went on, the more

111

depressed she became, and the worse she acted with men.

Finally, Jane was so depressed that she became suicidal, and attempted to take her own life by swallowing sleeping pills. Fortunately, she was caught in time by one of her girlfriends, received medical attention, and survived. Then, because the girlfriend insisted, and because she might have gotten into trouble with the police if she had not done so, she came for therapy.

In Jane's case what had to be done was not so much adjust her to any specific handicap, because she wasn't handicapped. She was in the average range of intelligence, and there was nothing wrong with her as far as appearance was concerned. Our goal was to get her adjusted to life *without unrealistic expectations,* such as had been fed to her year after year by her parents. She simply wasn't able to win the type of male she insisted she could be happily married to. Jane had to accept realistically that this was not the only type she could consider, that there were other human beings in the world, many of whom were attracted to her, and that perhaps it would be wiser if she lowered her sights and thought in terms of getting along with one of these individuals.

After several months of therapy Jane began to feel differently about herself and about her unrealistic aspirations. She became more attached to a man she had been seeing but whom she had never highly favored—because he was a plumber. Though this suitor was not stupid, he did little reading and was interested in baseball and other non-intellectual pursuits. He did seem to care for Jane and he was, in his way, very stable. I discussed with Jane her level of aspiration, and explained why it was not absolutely necessary that she adjust only to a bright professional person. As she started to rethink some of the earliest assumptions which had been inculcated by her parents, she became more attached to this suitor. Jane forgave him his occasional uncouthness and lack of intellectual ability. She began to make a healthy adjustment to him. Finally, she was propelled into an even deeper relationship. Her parents couldn't be cut off any longer, and insisted on visiting Jane in New York; she was so fearful that they would discover the type of life she had been leading that she pretended to have suddenly married the plumber. She went to live with him in his apartment, and allowed her parents to visit her there.

Jane's parents were scarcely enthusiastic about the man she had married. In a word, they were horrified. They began thinking of how to get the marriage annulled. But then they came to know the man and realized there was much to recommend about him.

At my request, I saw them and explained some of the facts of Jane's life, and how unlikely it was that she would ever marry the intellectual they desired. When the parents returned to their home, Jane continued living with this man. Later, they decided to marry.

Jane was through with her life as a call girl (of which her husband had known). As far as I can see, from my minor contacts with her since then, she had adjusted as well as could be expected to marriage.

When I last saw her, I asked her about her desire toward males, and whether she was ever tempted to go back to her former life, or be unfaithful to her husband. She admitted she thought about it occasionally, and once in a while even became mildly interested in another man. But there was no *compulsive* interest, in a nymphomaniacal sense, as there had been. So, as far as her compulsive sexual activity was concerned, she seemed to be cured. In other respects, she was having her problems but handled them reasonably well. Her parents seem to have fully accepted her husband now and they are happy that their daughter has settled down. Even though they never knew the details of her previous life, they always suspected that something was wrong.

These two cases, then, are examples of females who, largely because of training by their parents, were driven in a compulsive irrational manner to have promiscuous sex relations to obtain emotional but nonsexual satisfactions—satisfactions which were largely destructive.

There are various other ways—almost innumerable ways —in which parents can condition children to either rebelliously or conformingly engage in compulsive sexual behavior. A most important thing to note, however, is that it is not merely the parental conditioning which sets the stage for their children's ultimate behavior. Because, though it is most difficult for young children not to go along with the rules, attitudes and ideologies of their parents, a human being is the type of animal who can reassess values—and do something to change them.

The significant thing is that many of us who are strongly affected by parental conditioning, and who become disturbed in the process, do *not* reassess, reevaluate and change our early thinking pattern. Although it is possible for us to do this, it requires so much energy that, even when we see these patterns are leading us into ways of behavior that are truly self-defeating, we are loath to make the effort. Sometimes we don't realize that we *can* improve ourselves because we accept the attitude that we are doing badly in life and it is *impossible for us not to do badly*. We think we are truly worthless individuals, and doubt that we can do anything well. Sometimes we know fully we could do better if only we worked to change our patterns of living—but we refuse to work at it.

12

The Need to Be Loved

ONE OUTSTANDING REASON WHY A FEMALE IN OUR society becomes a nymphomaniac, unenjoyably driven to promiscuous sex relations, is because she has an overwhelming need to be loved, a hunger that generally seems to be greater in women than in men. Compelled by this drive to seek affection, security, and acceptance, she has a good many sexual experiences she might otherwise not desire.

We have already, in the opening chapter of this book, discussed Susan: unloved by her parents (or feeling unloved, and the feeling can have the same consequences as the reality), and permitting men to have intercourse with her in order to purchase affection from them. But Susan, perhaps untypical of the so-called nymphomaniac who indulges in sex relations with many men because she wants their love or approval, obtained practically no sexual satisfaction from such acts.

Probably most nymphomaniacs who engage in sex relations in search of love, at least secondarily receive a measure of sexual pleasure. Typical of this group is Mary Ann R.

MARY ANN R.

Mary Ann, when I first saw her, was thirty-two and married for the past five years to an artist. She had a two-year-old child, to whom she said she was quite devoted; she also said she got along rather well with her husband. He wasn't the best sex partner she had ever had, but they did have intercourse three or four times a week, according to her, and usually she obtained orgasm from the intercouse or the extravaginal play. Mary Ann was not complaining about her husband sexually, though at times he would go off on neurotic binges and not speak to her for days at a time. He would sulk, be unable to do his own work, and their sexual activity would diminish. But usually he did not neglect her.

Nonetheless, Mary Ann's problem was that she continued to be violently attracted to other men. When she met them socially, or when she sat next to them on a park bench while taking her baby for a stroll, she would begin to talk to the men, get involved and would soon be having sexual relations with them, she said, *against her own will*. Mary Ann did not want to destroy her marriage, and she feared that, if her husband discovered she was having these affairs, he would leave her. But she could not stop, even though she didn't particularly care for these sex partners.

What became clear, after I had seen Mary Ann for a few sessions, was that, though ostensibly she lusted after her pickup males, her abnormal sexual drive was a rationalization for the fact that she really wanted the emotional acquiescence of these men. She would look at a man and convince herself that he was good sexually, that she would get something from him she couldn't possibly get with her husband, and, compulsively, she would start an affair and soon find herself in bed with him. What actually seemed to be going on in her mind was that if she didn't somehow *win the approval* of this man, she was a worthless individual, who could not respect herself.

In other words, Mary Ann was one of those girls who prove the theory (George Herbert Mead, 1936, and Harry Stack Sullivan, 1947, 1953) that a human's self-estimation consists of the reflected appraisals of others. As did Susan, whose case we considered before, Mary Ann liked herself only when she was convinced that others liked her. She never stopped to challenge and question this belief, but accepted the fact that if others disapproved of her, she was doing something wrong and was contemptible. Consequently, if she even suspected that others, particularly men, did not accept her, she became frantic and had to do something quickly to gain their emotional allegiance.

What also happened, in Mary Ann's case, happens in many other cases of this nature: just because her husband *did* accept her, and she knew that he did, she no longer particularly favored him, nor valued his acceptance of her. That is, not basically liking herself and believing she was worthless, she depreciated anyone who accepted her consistently as her husband did, telling herself, "Because he likes a no-good like me, there must be something bad about *him*."

After convincing herself of this, no matter how consistently her husband approved of her, she would edit out this approval and feel that it meant absolutely nothing. Then she would have to go on to win the approval of some other individual of whom, before he accepted her, she would think very highly. But, once he did accept her, she would put the new lover in the same class as her husband (that is, an individual who was worthless *because he accepted her*), or she would tell herself, "Well, now that he accepts me, that's all right, but I have to make sure that others accept me, too."

To state this a little differently, Mary Ann needed, not only assurance that she was not bad, but she required continual reassurance *from one man after another* that she was good. Otherwise she would slide back to her basic estimation of herself: that she really wasn't worth troubling about. In her case, incidentally, she had *not* had an overcritical mother and father, but to the contrary had ultra-approving parents who said everything she did was glorious, and indicated she would always have to live up to that standard. Mary Ann just *had* to be Queen of the May—especially in the public eye. As a result, when she was not proving herself to others and thereby reassuring herself, she became terribly self-depreciatory.

Once her marriage was a settled-down affair, and there was nothing new in the form of approval to be gained by it, Mary Ann began this pattern of meeting new men every few weeks, to be sure that she attracted them both physically and mentally. As soon as she got into bed with them, she tried to get them to tell her she was an interesting person to talk to and one of the best bed partners they had ever had. She was an attractive girl, and had no trouble finding new partners; she gained an adeptness at bedmanship which made her even more attractive to most of the males with whom she had sex relations.

Mary Ann's postmarital sexual pattern was something of a replica of the premarital one. In her late teens and early twenties, she lived away from home and was active in artistic circles. In those days she seldom spent a night away from a male. She seemed afraid to be by herself, and arranged her life never to be alone.

As we went more and more into her problems in the course of the therapeutic sessions, it became clear that the reason Mary Ann was unwilling to be by herself, was because then she had *nothing to do but think*. She would begin thinking negatively about what she hadn't done in life, hadn't been a great poet, hadn't won the finest man in the world, and so on. She would think back to her lack of success in these areas, and always end by castigating herself severely. When she was with other people, she could concentrate on talking about her problems to them, having some interchange

117

which would get her away from self-criticism. Or, she would manage to have them assure her she was not as bad as she thought she was.

Compulsively Mary Ann not only had sexual relations with a man, but she had to spend the night in the same bed with him so as not to be alone, not to have time to think. She had followed this pattern before marriage; and now after marriage, not having to seek a bed partner, she continued to look for the verbal reassurance that she received from men, and which, in her mind, was usually connected with having an affair with them. She won praise from her partners for being sexually adept, and she somehow was usually able to discuss her problems and obtain reassurance from the men, as she had before her marriage: she was a pretty girl, she was intelligent, she probably did have talent, and if she only kept at some of the things she wanted to do, she would finally succeed.

In Mary Ann's case, I was able to show her that most of her compulsive sexual activity did not stem from pronounced sex desires, but from her need to be approved and accepted by men. I was also able to work with her in attacking the ideology which led to her compulsive behavior. For it is a basic tenet of rational-emotive psychotherapy (The form of psychotherapy which I practice these days, previously having practiced a fairly classical kind of psychoanalysis and, later, psychoanalytically-oriented psychotherapy) that *insight is not enough*. Showing a patient exactly how and when she became disturbed about something that now upsets her is all very interesting, and may prove helpful to her because she then *may* be able to change her basic ideology which led to, and keeps causing, the disturbance.

It has been shown by many other psychotherapeutic theorists, including Franz Alexander (Alexander and French, 1946), who previously was classical psychoanalytic, that patients not only have to see the basic philosophic concepts and assumptions which they employ to upset themselves, but they must also forcefully, vigorously, and consistently challenge and question these ideologies in order to get them to change (Berne, 1961; Diaz-Guerrera, 1959; Dubois, 1907; Grimes, 1961; Phillips, 1956).

In rational-emotive psychotherapy, the principles of which have been expounded in a series of recent books and articles (Ellis, 1957, 1962a, 1962b, 1963a, 1963b; Ellis and Harper, 1961a, 1961b) the patient is first shown that her problems stem not from what has happened in her past history but

118

from philosophies of life derived from this history. These philosophies of life are then vigorously challenged and tackled until they are changed.

In Mary Ann's case, she was shown that she was telling herself two basic sets of internalized ideas or philosophic assumptions—first a sane, and then an insane set. The *sane* internalized phrases, paragraphs, sentences which Mary Ann was telling herself were of the nature of, "When I do badly —that is, when I don't do the things in life which I would like to do—this is deplorable. I would rather do well, and I'm not doing well, and that is too bad."

Then *should* have followed a set of sane sentences: "All right! Since I am doing badly at the present time, what can I do in the future? How can I change my thinking and my work procedure so as to improve?"

Instead of telling herself these sane sentences, Mary Ann, like most disturbed people, began to tell herself a second set of *irrational* sentences, of the nature, "Now that I see I am doing badly, and not doing the things I would really like to do, this is terrible, this is awful, and this proves that I am no good as a person. Not only is my behavior poor, but *I* am no good, *I* am worthless; and I am presumably *incapable* of changing this behavior, because I am worthless."

This second set of ideas, those that Mary Ann was internalizing, was irrational because *it did not follow* from the first set. If a human being is doing badly at the moment, it *could* mean she is incapable of doing well and is actually an inadequate individual who cannot possibly do better in the future; but it could *also* mean nothing of the sort. It could mean she has not yet had the experience to do well, and therefore is doing badly; or it could signify that she is quite capable of doing well, but she *thinks* she isn't able and *therefore* doesn't really try to do better.

The irrational element in Mary Ann's internalized ideas was not the notion that she was doing badly, but that because she was doing badly at the moment, she could not possibly do better in the future. This type of belief is metaphysical, in a sense, because it is essentially unprovable. It's impossible to prove that a person who has not done well to date cannot possibly do well in the future. To reach this conclusion, therefore, is to accept an unvalidatable set of assumptions.

Moreover, Mary Ann's second set of internalized ideas were irrational because they say that, *if* she is doing badly, and *if* she cannot do better in the future, she is a worthless individual for being this inadequate. Not this idea (that if a human being *is* inadequate, he or she is therefore a worthless

119

individual) is completely unprovable for the simple reason that it is totally definitional. There is no reason why an inadequate person has to be conceived as a worthless person, except by arbitrary, moralistic evaluation.

Thus, a mother who has a mentally deficient child may consider the child worthless just because she is mentally deficient; or she may decide that despite this deficiency, she still loves her child and considers her to be a worthwhile human being whom she will try to help in any possible way. Therefore she can define this handicapped child either as worthless or as good. By the same token, this child herself, assuming she is capable of some thinking, can define herself as utterly valueless because many people define her as such, and because they do not wish to have much to do with her. Or, she can *accept* this deficiency (and whatever other disabilities she may happen to have), and define herself as an individual who is handicapped *but still worthwhile*, still capable of enjoying herself and having a good life.

Moreover, as is explained in *Reason and Emotion in Psychotherapy* (Ellis, 1962a), there is no reason why a person must accept her *extrinsic* value, that is, the value she has to other people, and there is no reason why she should make it the same as intrinsic value, that is, the value she places on herself.

Though the people you know may think you are inadequate, incompetent, or worthless, it is still possible for you to accept yourself and to like yourself, as long as (a) you are alive, and (b) there is some possibility of finding aspects of life you can enjoy. Your extrinsic value depends upon what *other people* think of you, and may vary enormously from place to place, from time to time. As a result of this variation, it cannot be categorically tied to your intrinsic value, except by arbitrary definition (Hartman, 1959, 1961; Thorne, 1961; Tillich, 1953).

To get back to the case of Mary Ann, I was able to show her that even if she never became what she wished to be in life—if she were not an outstanding poet, for example, and never did any of the other things she would like to do—that would not mean she was worthless. It meant only that she wasn't able to do what she would like to do, and that maybe she would be a little less happy than she might otherwise be; *but she'd still have plenty of room for enjoyment in life.*

I was able to convince Mary Ann that no matter what others thought of her, she did not have to accept *their* evaluation of her as her own evaluation of herself. Not that she should completely ignore others' criticism. If she were doing something outlandish, and people brought this to her attention, she might ask herself, "Am I behaving correctly?" and might well reply to herself that she was not. When, however, others devalued her *as a person* for being mistaken, she need not conclude, "I *am* worthless." She might sanely conclude, "Since I am mistaken and I am doing badly, how can I do better next time? If I *can* do better, fine. If I can't, if I really *am* incompetent at doing what these people would like me to do, and if there's no possibility of my pleasing them—*too bad.* I can live reasonably well with my intrinsic inadequacies; and I do not have to consider myself a villainess for having limitations."

At this point in treatment, as happens with so many of my patients, Mary Ann started to do many of the things she had avoided before.

Mary Ann began to write; she produced more poetry in the next few weeks than she had written in the previous few years. Although all of it didn't come out as well as she wished, she continued writing and did gain satisfaction from what she had done. She was so preoccupied with this that her dire-felt necessity to have others approve of her was reduced. The less she *needed* to be accepted by others, the more she was able to accept herself and to refrain from compulsively seeking the favors of men.

Mary Ann started to become preoccupied with writing for its sake, focusing on the task or the problem of the poetry, rather than on the acclaim she hoped to get by doing it. She began to be task-centered, or problem-centered, rather than self-centered. (Incidentally, the term *self-centered* is really a misnomer, since, boiled down to its essentials it usually means "I am interested in myself only if I can gain the interest of others in me." Therefore, it's actually a synonym for the term *other-directed*, which is used by David Riesman (1953) and other sociological and psychological thinkers.) So Mary Ann was able to become much less other-directed as we tackled, challenged, and questioned her basic philosophy of defining herself as good only in terms of what others found in her.

As she became more and more interested in her own creative productivity, Mary Ann lost her intense need to have others, both males and females, interested in her. This is not to say she did not appreciate the approval of others. When men and women found her personally attractive, or found that her work was good, she enjoyed their approval. But she no longer felt *compelled* to have others accept her.

121

Along with losing this dire need for love, Mary Ann, quite to her surprise, lost practically all her compulsive sexual interest in males. From time to time she saw an attractive man and quietly asked herself, "Well, might it not be nice to be in bed with him?" But this was just an idle question, and didn't really mean anything to her. There was no strong impulse to go to bed with him, and no urgent sensation in her genital region, which she previously experienced when she was interested in the approval of a man.

Within a few months after first being seen for rational-emotive psychotherapy, Mary Ann's compulsive hypersexuality had completely disappeared. She was still a reasonably high-sexed woman, and now tended to enjoy her husband for five or six times a week rather than the three or four times that she had previously. Occasionally, in bed with him, she would think of some male she had met that day, or who was a friend of hers; and at times she would even envision having sex relations with another man. But this was the extent to which her promiscuity would go. Otherwise, she was satisfied with her husband, and was now able to build an emotional relationship with him on a sounder basis than she had ever been able to do.

Mary Ann's case is that of a woman who really was reasonably highly sexed and could enjoy promiscuous relations, but was compulsively driven to them because of her strong need for approval. This is a fairly typical cause of compulsive hypersexuality in woman.

This is not to say that all, or most, nymphomaniacs are driven by their love needs. There are other reasons why a woman, without necessarily having a physiological compulsion to promiscuity, may be a sexually indiscriminate person and may do many things of which her society does not approve. Nonetheless, a large percentage of compulsive sexually driven women are motivated by *basically nonsexual*, but highly amative needs. It isn't that these women have an overwhelming need to love; it is a need to *be* loved.

In extreme cases this desire may even take the form of erotomania, a severe manifestation in which the woman not only convinces herself she must be loved by a certain man, but that he absolutely *does* love her. Actually, in most of these cases, the man is only mildly interested in the woman or perhaps even dislikes her; yet, she convinces herself he is utterly, madly in love with her—and in many instances she incessantly bothers him. In some of these cases the man who is chosen is a well-known individual who has hardly heard of the woman with whom he is supposed to be in love; in other cases, he's just an ordinary individual whom she has met and who she insists is devoted to her, when actually he has hardly given her any thought. Erotomania is a rare disorder, and is usually a manifestation of psychosis.

Often a woman, instead of, or in addition to, having a dire need to *be* loved, will have an abnormally strong need to love. In this case she starts falling in love with males who are unsuitable for her in terms of intelligence or social station. A common motivation for this compulsive behavior is that the woman, consciously or unconsciously, expects her love will be returned; *it frequently is* if she behaves—and loves—in a pleasing manner. It could be said there is method in her madness.

Another common motivation is that the woman is so convinced she can do virtually nothing in life but love, that she devotes herself in a preoccupied manner to this behavior. For example, there is the woman who would really like to be a scientist but who is so convinced of her feelings of inadequacy that she may deliberately (though often unconsciously) select a less disciplined field such as love. There is, to her mind, a much greater chance at succeeding in this endeavor than in some more competitive and difficult activity. Here, once again, the woman's underlying feelings of inadequacy drive her into a field at which she has some propensity and in which, to some degree, she enjoys participating, but which really is not as satisfying as it would appear.

To sum up what we have been saying: Nymphomania, like almost all other forms of human disturbance, is largely derivative of a person's low estimation of herself. Believing that she must be outstanding, and feeling that she would not be able, she tends to use her sexuality, which she has found attractive to men, to gain acceptance and approval—and thereby, temporarily, to relieve the underlying feeling that she is no good.

When she is thus compulsively driven to try to raise her self-confidence, a woman bogs herself down in the usual vicious circle traveled by people who try to raise their self-esteem by winning others' approval. *True* self-confidence does not, as most of us falsely assume, consist of doing well or knowing that other people like you. Rather, it consists largely of *liking yourself* and considering yourself worthwhile *whether or not other people approve of you.* Consequently,

123

women who try to build their confidence by gaining approval, achieve only a Pyrrhic victory. Underneath, they still fear that they cannot possibly win everyone's love (which, of course they can't), so they do not *truly* like themselves.

Each "victory" they win does not give them basic satisfaction, and they feel compulsively driven to the next—and to the next—so-called victory.

The intense need to be loved and approved can only be tackled on a philosophic basis. Because it is the *idea,* the *concept* that one must be accepted by others in order to be worthwhile, which has to be uprooted. If this is not eliminated, it leads to more and more aberrant behavior. If, however, this dire need to be loved is forcefully challenged, if a woman is able to ask herself: *"Why* do I have to be approved by others in order to like myself? Why is it necessary for me to be a success, a leader, to think of myself as a valuable human being?"—she will eventually see that there is no reason why she should not like herself whether or not other people do. When this realization is attained, then, and then only, the abnormal need to be loved vanishes, to be replaced by the normal desire for approval.

Nothing is probably more normal in human existence than our feeling of satisfaction and pleasure when other people like us. For it is good, practically and generally, to be approved by others. They will do many things for us that they will not do if they do not approve of us. A woman who is loved by men will be able to obtain companionship, sex pleasure, economic support, etc., by being thus approved. And it would be silly to say, as some do, that it doesn't matter *at all* whether or not men accept this woman. It *does* matter. *There is such a thing as practical love,* or love that leads to practical good results for the person who is loved. And it would be foolish for a woman not to try to be accepted to some extent, to achieve some of these results.

Moreover, the feeling of loving itself is a more pleasurable emotion and has many beneficial effects. Even when being loved does not really help a woman get what she truly wants out of life, her loving will normally result in a more creative life which will give her much satisfaction. It would be foolish to denigrate the value she might receive from this love.

When, moreover, a woman loves, she certainly prefers reciprocation of her feelings. It is possible for her to love without reciprocation and still to gain satisfaction. This, however, is unusual.

There is nothing in the least wrong, therefore, in a wom-

124

an's preferring returned love. It is when she feels that she *must* have reciprocation, and feels that she is a failure as a human being when she does not receive it, that she finds herself in emotional difficulties. And these emotional difficulties, as we have demonstrated in the present chapter, constitute one of the prime reasons for females becoming compulsively promiscuous.

13

The Treadmill
of Nymphomania

WE HAVE ALREADY SEEN THE PATTERN OF SOME CON-
quering women, those female counterparts to the Don Juan:
the Donna Juanitas. There was Dolores, scarred as a child,
who found it constantly necessary to reaffirm her ability to
attract men. And Isabel, plagued by self-doubt and feelings
of intellectual inadequacy, out to show she was more than
adequate in another area of human endeavor.

For the conquering woman, society offers a double trap.
First, she is brought up in a man's world, where economic
and cultural opportunities for the male far exceed those for
the female, and where she is regarded as "the second sex."
To assert her equality with men, she often feels compelled to
establish her superiority. To show that she is not subdued, she
may feel obliged to prove herself the dominant one—and the
conqueror.

And then, if this conquest takes on sexual forms, she is
ostracized and may even be punished—while males indulging
in similar activity are treated leniently. It is a sad commen-
tary on our sexual mores that when a male in our society is
highly promiscuous, nothing is done about it. In fact, his
peers usually look up to him, they envy him; but when a
female behaves in a similar fashion, she is scorned, and, if
young, often taken in hand by the authorities. Every effort is
made to have her *condemn herself* and to accept society's
view that she is a tramp.

A few of these women, as described previously, do continue their ceaseless conquests for many years, even after the
usual age of retirement. Nymphomaniacs driven by a need to
conquer are unlike these having a need for love; the latter
mainly subscribe to *Irrational Idea No. 1* while the former—the Donna Juanitas—largely follow *Irrational Idea No.
2*. Irrational Idea No. 1, discussed earlier, and analyzed in
detail in the books *Reason and Emotion in Psychotherapy*
(Ellis, 1962a) and *A Guide to Rational Living* (Ellis and

Harper, 1962a) is the dire necessity for an adult human being to be loved or approved by virtually *every person* in her community. Irrational Idea No. 2 is the idea that a woman should be thoroughly competent and achieving in *all possible respects* if she is to consider herself worthwhile.

Irrational Idea No. 1 leads to the nymphomaniacal behavior described in the preceding chapter; this idea will frequently drive the woman to have sex relations in order to be approved, accepted or loved by the man. Irrational Idea No. 2, which overlaps with No. 1, is a similar notion applied to oneself. In other words, "I can only love myself if I do remarkably well in every respect, and therefore prove that I am worthwhile."

Behind Irrational Idea No. 2 is the same thinking as underlies Irrational Idea No. 1, since the reason I think that I have to do well in every respect in order to love myself is, in the final analysis, because other people also think so, and they would only love me if I were competent and adequate in all respects. *At least, this is what I believe.* People might accept me even if I am not competent in all respects. But the general tendency in most human societies is for people to be competent, and therefore I believe that I *must* be competent in order to get them to do so. By extending this idea, I may end up with the assumption that no matter what other people think of me, I, in my own right, must be adequate or else I cannot possibly respect myself.

The first type of nymphomaniac is driven to many beds mainly because she would consider herself worthless if she were not *loved* by many males; and the second type is driven to promiscuity because she would not like herself if she were not *adequate*. By being a good sexual partner to men, she proves to herself that she had a degree of adequacy. Neither of these groups of females, of course, is motivated by what it wants to do. The motivation is what they think, at bottom, others would like them to do. They are, as noted before, essentially other-directed and distinctly disturbed.

A *nondisturbed* woman would ask herself "What do I really want out of life, and how can I get what I want? I don't *desire* people to hate me while I'm getting what I want. I prefer them to be friendly. But if they are going to dislike me or disapprove of me, and that's the only way I can get what I desire, that's too bad. I first have to go after what I want." The *disturbed* person, on the other hand, is primarily interested in what other people wish her to do, and she sells her soul over and over again. And the nymphomaniac sells her soul by selling her body.

Again, it must be stressed that not all nymphomaniacs are

127

in the groups we have discussed; there are other groups which we will discuss later. But promiscuity, with its compulsive aspect, does tend to result from some irrational basic idea or philosophy of life that the individual holds. *All* forms of compulsivity tend to stem from such thinking. The compulsive individual instead of saying: "I would like to do this, let's see how I can do it," is saying *"I must do* this and it is terrible, horrible, and awful if I don't."

More specifically, the nymphomaniac is not telling herself, "I would like to go to bed and have sex relations with this particular man, perhaps enjoy the sex act, and maybe even more than that, achieve a good amative marital relationship." She is telling herself, "I must go to bed with this man, because if I don't do so, he might not like me—and I coudn't stand that." Or: "I might not be able to prove my competence as a potential sex partner, and I couldn't stand *that.*" So the compulsive is driven by necessity to have sex relations, and has them on a *relatively* nonpleasurable basis.

The noncompulsive, normal individual *wishes* to have sex relations at times, and has them; but a healthy person can also do without them when they are not available or when it is impractical to have them. The compulsive cannot wait for practicality. She finds herself forced to do impractical or self-defeating acts because she thinks she is utterly worthless and cannot exist if she doesn't perform them. *A compulsive, a nymphomaniac, is a disturbed person who should be understood, first, as disturbed* and only secondly as sexually promiscuous. Her promiscuity is but a function of her disturbance, and does not by any means cause it. The promiscuity may reinforce her neurosis or psychosis—because, once she becomes promiscuous, she may then blame herself for being indiscriminate and thereby become even more disturbed.

This does not mean that all *promiscuous* females are necessarily compulsive, and therefore disturbed. *Some highly-sexed and unselective women are exactly that, and nothing more.* They are women who have an enormous amount of sexual drive, frequently but not always on a hormonal or other physiological basis, who feel uncomfortable when they are not having sex relations. These women are physically driven, to a mild degree, but are well within the normal range.

14

Compulsivity

COMPULSIVITY IS THE BASIC ELEMENT IN NYMPHO-
mania. It is part of the definition; if it is not present, we are
dealing with a *different* problem: controlled promiscuity. In
the one case, there is emotional illness; in the other there is
socially condemned *but not sick* behavior.

However, in some instances, as discussed earlier, the woman becomes a nymphomaniac because she is generally compulsive. These individuals are fixed on their symptoms; their
entire attitude toward life, usually from earliest childhood, is
distorted and bizarre. In most instances these borderline
psychotic individuals have exceptionally low ego-strength.
They do not like themselves, they demand of themselves that
they be absolutely perfect, and when they are not they
belabor themselves mercilessly. At the same time, they often
will not accept anyone else whose behavior isn't perfect. In
other words, *they are exceptionally moralistic*; they not only
try to do well, or try to get others to do well, they demand
perfection from themselves and other individuals—and they
strongly condemn themselves and others for not living up to
these impossible demands.

My experience over many years with such individuals has
led me to believe that it is not only that they are raised to be
the way they are, but that there is also a distinct *biological*
element in their disturbance. They are afflicted with some
kind of cognitive slippage, as authorities have increasingly
pointed out in recent years (Meehl, 1962); this cognitive
slippage probably results from an inborn tendency to think
crookedly. Now this doesn't mean that these individuals cannot, under any circumstances, think straight; but they do find
it difficult to make the subtle discriminations needed to get
along in life, especially in interpersonal relationships. Because it is most difficult for borderline psychotics to make
subtle discriminations, they have to be laboriously and rigor-
ously trained to do this, practically require blueprints for

living, and have to be corrected over and over again until they learn to correct some obvious errors and learn how to live a saner life.

This training is a difficult process; I believe it cannot be done with the usual forms of passive, nondirective therapy, or even in psychoanalytic psychotherapy where the emphasis is usually on showing the individual how she originally became disturbed and how the original trauma is related to the present. Psychotics and borderline psychotics must be clearly and consistently taught better philosophies of life, and taught how to think more scientifically. This teaching is best done in a very active-directive manner, with the therapist continually participating rather than just passively listening or reflecting the patient's feelings. The therapist must go over, and over again, some of the major points until the patient finally sees exactly what she is doing that causes her to think and act ineffectually, and sees how she can change her self-defeating behavior.

What is more, as has been noted in several recent writings on rational-emotive psychotherapy (Ellis, 1962a, 1962b, 1962c; 1963a, 1963b, 1963c), the therapist cannot, non-directively, leave it to the patients to use the insights which they gain in therapy. It is far better to give them direct *homework assignments*, with the therapist concretely following up to see that these assignments are carried out. The patients are taught in practice, in the reality of their own lives rather than in the confines of the therapeutic relationship, to act in a saner and more rational manner.

JANICE W.

As an example of the homework assignments often given in rational-emotive psychotherapy, we can take the case of Janice W. Janice was a severely disturbed woman who had been institutionalized twice: once at the age of seventeen, for a year, and once again at the age of twenty-three, for an eight-month period. She had been diagnosed as a paranoid schizophrenic; she felt everybody was against her, that people were scheming to hurt her. This patient was a nymphomaniac in the sense that she compulsively slept with many men. Usually she had an affair for only a few weeks—and then insisted the man was spying on her, reading her letters, appointment book, and diary. Janice felt her lovers did these things to expose her, to see what a terrible person she was. As soon as they became suspicious, she had to get away. She would accuse them of behavior of which, as far as one could tell, they were not guilty. Either she left them in a huff, or they left her.

This went on and on; Janice went from one man to another, and soon lost each lover. At each separation, she felt depressed and was sure she was worthless because she had lost another man. When, occasionally, she realized she had been oversuspicious, she blamed herself for that, too, and became even more depressed. So it went, in a typical vicious circle.

The one thing Janice kept insisting was that she had to leave most of her lovers because the tension kept mounting—they spied on her, and she was forced to tell them what she thought, and to destroy the relationship. I insisted that this was not necessarily the case, and kept asking her why she couldn't tolerate the tension. All she could do was to say, "It makes me feel terrible, and I just can't stand it; there's something about it that is just too tense."

What that something was she could never say, but she was sure it existed. I finally said to her, "All right! You say there's something you can't stand, can't put your finger on. Now I'm going to give you a very definite homework assignment with your new boyfriend. You just met him last week. Your assignment is to stay with him for a minimum of three weeks, and say absolutely nothing even though you're positive he is spying on you—reading your diaries, going through your letters, or looking at your appointment book. You must say absolutely nothing to him about this during the next three weeks. *Just let your tension mount!* Then we'll be able to be more specific and to see what the tension is."

Janice was extremely reluctant to do this. She tried to argue that it couldn't be done. She even considered leaving therapy to avoid doing it. But I said, "Now, look: there's no other way. You're very vague, and only by cornering you, and by letting you experience some of the pain of the tension mounting, will we be able to pin down its source. So I'm giving you this as a homework assignment."

Again she tried to resist, but I said, "Well, there's going to have to be a choice. Either you're going to do this assignment, or we're just not going to get anywhere in therapy; so you might as well quit, as you've been thinking of doing."

Janice trusted me at this time because I didn't give her any nonsense (as several of her previous therapists had done). She didn't want to lose me, so she finally agreed to the assignment.

For the next week and a half, during which time I saw her for extra sessions (patients are usually seen only once a week for rational-emotive therapy, unless they are in the throes of an acute disturbance), she kept reporting that the tension was mounting and mounting—and she still couldn't put her finger on it. She vigorously refrained, in accordance with her assignment, from saying anything to her boyfriend about her suspicions. Finally the tension became intolerable. Janice couldn't say *what* was becoming more intolerable, but she kept saying, "It's so nervewracking. I'm going to crack, something in me is going to break if I don't open my mouth and tell him my suspicions."

I said, "You'll just have to go on. You certainly *can* look at those sentences you're telling yourself and find out what they are. Now, go on until you drive yourself to look at those sentences."

Like many of my patients, Janice was lackadaisical at considering the simpler exclamatory sentences with which she kept creating her disturbance. Finally, after a week or so she reported her tension was mounting higher and higher—and the assignment still wasn't finished. I said to her, "Now look, you're still vague about this. There must be something there. What is it, what exactly are you telling yourself to create the tension?"

Although she couldn't spontaneously come up with the answer, by responding to my questions she began, indirectly, to tell me what was bothering her. Somewhat to my surprise, and to hers, we found that what was plaguing her was not the thought: "If he continues spying on me, he's going to find out, and he will leave me." Rather, it was: "If he goes on spying on me this way he may find me out, and *still* may accept me. He may not do anything about it, but he might like me in spite of these terrible things he may find out about me. If he accepts me on this basis, *he* must be no good. I am inferior; if he can accept such an individual, then that puts him on the same lowly plane and I cannot respect him any longer."

So what Janice was really afraid of was that she would not be able to respect her boyfriend any longer, and then find herself in the bind that *no man* could be good for her. Either he would find her out—and leave her; or, he would find her out and *not* leave her—in which case she couldn't respect him and she would have to leave him.

That left absolutely zero males available for Janice. She was so afraid to find this out that the tension kept mounting, as she stayed with one man, and it finally forced her to leave him, usually very early in the game. In a sense she was prophylactically, in advance, taking what she considered a

132

lesser evil. She was accustomed to considering herself worthless, and was adjusted to *that*. But she was not in the least used to the idea that a man might accept her as a worthless being—and then he would be utterly worthless, *and there would be nothing, absolutely nothing else for her in the whole world*.

Anyway, Janice's homework assignment graphically brought out the ideas with which she kept indoctrinating herself. After this, I was able to do what I normally do with my patients: that is, not only show what is bothering them by giving them insight into the past and the present, but also to tackle, vigorously and directly, those life philosophies which are revealed. In Janice's case, the philosophy attacked was the idea of the nonacceptance of a presumably bad person; i.e., if Janice were no good and her lover accepted her, *he* would then be unacceptable.

I tried to show Janice that no human being is really ever to blame (in the sense of being totally worthless); although humans are frequently responsible for their acts and should be helped to act better in the future. If she were not to blame, then her lover was not to blame for failing to note her flaws or for accepting her despite the flaws. I worked, and worked, with her for the next several weeks on this problem, getting Janice to see that neither she nor her boyfriends were to blame for their errors, that people make mistakes, because that's what *humanness* is—fallibility, the proneness to make mistakes. But people can actually be acceptable *with* their mistakes. There's nothing desirable about mistake-making, though it has its interesting aspects. The world would be terribly dull if none of us ever made errors. Nonetheless, while you can dislike an individual's mistakes, you don't have to hate *him*. He is not a terrible *person* for erring, even though his errors may be reprehensible.

We worked for a good many weeks on getting Janice to accept herself when she made a mistake, and to accept other human beings, especially her boyfriends, when they blundered. When she finally was able to do this—to see that even if she were one of the worst mistake-makers in the world, she would not be a louse, and if her boyfriend cavalierly glossed over her mistakes and accepted her, he would not be a bum—her tensions started to disappear; she was able to stay with her current boyfriend for several months. She did eventually part with him, due to other incompatibilities.

After a year of treatment, Janice moved to another city and found a better job. When I last saw her she was, for the first time in her life, not only remaining attached to a male, after living with him for a year, but she was planning the future with him. At this time, I would not say she was totally cured, since paranoid schizophrenics, such as she, may rarely be considered cured, even when they are significantly improved and are getting along in society. But for Janice her compulsive promiscuity had ended. She was able to have longer relationships with males, and to enjoy them both sexually and amatively on this more enduring basis. In this sense, her therapy did lead to a reasonably successful conclusion.

To summarize what has been said in this chapter: There are many reasons why females are likely to become compulsive nymphomaniacs, and most of these involve basic *irrational ideas* such as the dire need to be loved and the need to conquer other human beings; these irrational ideas cause various symptoms of serious disturbance, such as phobias, obsessions and compulsions, psychosomatic symptoms and other emotional aberrations. *Nymphomania is not basically different in this respect from other emotional ailments, and it has the same causes.*

This group of nymphomaniacs definitely can be helped to overcome their compulsive promiscuity. But whether most of them can be completely cured is dubious for, as I have said previously, borderline psychosis and outright psychosis may well have biological as well as psychological causes, and even successful love and sex life, even though they are not totally when the latter are eliminated, a basic biological deficit may remain. Nevertheless, psychotherapy can be of enormous benefit to these people, and they can live comfortably in the community, go about their work, and have some form of successful love and sex life, even though they are not totally normal.

PART FOUR

Treatment

15

The Irrationality of Human Disturbances

NYMPHOMANIACS DIFFER FROM HEALTHY, SEXUALLY active women in that these compulsively promiscuous women have usually internalized several if not all of the basic irrational ideas and concepts of human society, and the therapist as well as the patient must become aware of these irrationalities if they are to be effectively attacked.

These irrational ideas, referred to earlier in this book and discussed in *Reason and Emotion in Psychotherapy* (Ellis, 1962a) and in *A Guide to Rational Living* (Ellis and Harper, 1961a), are as follows:

Irrational Idea No. 1. It is essential for an adult human being to be loved and approved by virtually every significant person in his community.

Irrational Idea No. 2. One should be thoroughly competent, adequate, and achieving in all possible respects if one is to consider oneself worthwhile.

Irrational Idea No. 3. Certain people are bad, wicked, or villainous, that they should be severely blamed and punished for their villainy.

Irrational Idea No. 4. It is terrible and catastrophic when things are not the way that one would very much like them to be.

Irrational Idea No. 5. Human happiness is externally

135

caused and people have little or no ability to control their sorrows and disturbances.

Irrational Idea No. 6. If something is, or may be, dangerous, one should be terribly concerned about it, and should keep dwelling on the possibility of its occurring.

Irrational Idea No. 7. It is easier to avoid than to face certain life difficulties and self-responsibilities.

Irrational Idea No. 8. One should be dependent on others; and, one needs someone stronger than oneself on whom to rely.

Irrational Idea No. 9. One's past history is an all-important determiner of one's personal behavior, and because something once strongly affected one's life, it should indefinitely have a similar effect.

Irrational Idea No. 10. One should become quite upset over other people's problems and disturbances.

Irrational Idea No. 11. There is invariably a right, precise and perfect solution to human problems and it is catastrophic if this perfect solution is not found.

These ideas can be somewhat condensed into two basic concepts. These concepts are: (*a*) the highly irrational notion that, in order to be a good or worthwhile individual in one's own right, one must be loved by other people, and/or be a highly achieving person; and (*b*) the irrational idea that when one doesn't get exactly what one wants in the world (that is to say, when one is frustrated), it is horrible and catastrophic, and one cannot possibly be happy.

Still another way to summarize these basic irrational ideas is to say that blame is the essence of human disturbance. Thus, if (*a*) one blames oneself for doing anything, no matter how wrong or mistaken or erroneous it may be, or (*b*) if one blames other human beings for their mistakes and errors, one then *must* become anxious and/or angry and hostile. *Anxiety and hostility are the essence of human disturbances.*

Are there any other basic irrational ideas that lead to emotional illness? Possibly there are, though in the last decade of working with the eleven basic ideas outlined above, I and my associates, who are now fairly numerous throughout the country, have not as yet come up with a new irrational idea which cannot somehow be subsumed under one of the basic eleven. I have never found an emotionally disturbed human being who was not severely blaming himself or somebody else for his assumed or actual wrong behavior. It is our

136

contention, therefore, that nymphomaniacs, like other human beings, have these basic irrational ideas, and when they are compulsively and non-enjoyable promiscuous, they are doing so as a result of firmly believing, consciously or unconsciously, in one or more of these basic irrationalities.

Now this is not to say that all people who are *called* nymphomaniacs are seriously disturbed and have irrational philosophies. Many so-called nymphomaniacs are nothing but highly-sexed females acting in a promiscuous manner (by the standards of our society), and who are scorned for this. Many of them are more in the normal range of emotion than are those inhibited females who are not doing what they wish, sexually. Others, the *true* nymphomaniacs (as defined in the first chapter), have some physiological disorder and are driven by their *physical* problem to compulsive hypersexuality and to sex-love relations whether or not they truly enjoy them.

If we omit the highly-sexed women who are not aberrant in any way, and if we omit those *true or endogenous* nymphomaniacs, then the remaining women are nymphomaniacs who engage in promiscuous sex relations on a driven, non-enjoyable basis. These women are invariably beset by one or more of the major irrational ideas we have just delineated. In therapy, they must not only be shown that they have these ideas, but they should have a therapist who actively, forthrightly, directly and forcefully attacks their silly notions—until they finally give them up.

These then, are the basic causes of nymphomania, and this method of getting at a woman's basic philosophy of life —challenging and questioning it until it changes—can help the nymphomaniac to take the road to mental health.

16

*Why Rational-Emotive
Therapy?*

PSYCOTHERAPY IS SHARPLY DIVIDED ON THE TECHNIQUE for alleviating the emotional distress of the nymphomaniac. Let us look at some of the *classical methods,* and see what they contribute and where they are found wanting.

Psychoanalytic methods of treatment. According to Sigmund Freud and his main followers, compulsive promiscuity usually arises because a woman has been traumatized, or badly conditioned, early in her childhood, has not gained a true sexual maturity, and remains fixated on some pregenital or nocoital level—and, therefore, is not able to be fully satisfied sexually. According to this theory, a woman can be helped to overcome her nymphomania by intensive classical psychoanalysis, in the course of which she free-associates for hundreds of sessions, has her dreams analyzed, becomes involved in intensive transference relationship with the therapist—through which she can learn to relate adequately to males and not view them as if they were a punitive father or a negative mother, thereby resolving early traumatic conditioning and becoming sexually mature.

For a few years I tried this psychoanalytic method of treatment with nymphomaniacs and found it had some measure of efficacy. When I explained to my female patients that they were upset *today* about some of the attitudes and ideas they had derived from their parents early in childhood, and that they need no longer be upset by these ideas, they were able to overcome their nymphomania to some degree. I found, however, that there were a number of instances in which this was not true; no matter how detailed the insight into the early trauma was, and regardless of how clearly the female seemed to understand the origins of her disturbance, she still did not improve. Sometimes she would ask, "Dr. Ellis, now that I see exactly why I have become a nymphomaniac and what is bothering me, why don't I change?" I would give her the classical answers that she still did not want to get better, or she was resisting me or didn't truly understand the origin of her disturbance. Often I would convince her that this was so; but *I* wasn't thoroughly convinced.

I looked around for a more effective method of treatment and, finally, developed my present method of rational-emotive psychotherapy. I have found this much more effective in my treatment of nymphomaniacs and practically all other kinds of emotionally disturbed persons.

ADDIE F.

I was particularly jolted in this respect several years ago when I had one nymphomaniac patient who agreed that we had found precisely the origins of her disturbance. Although Addie F. at first denied any childhood sex experience, when we went deeper into the analysis of her early life and into several of her dreams, this patient broke through and remembered that for several months, when she was about eleven or twelve years of age, and apparently already pubscent, an uncle had started coming into her room and having abortive sex relations with her. He would come to her after she was already in bed, lie in bed with his clothes on, and talk to her. He would then rub up against her buttocks until a convulsive movement of his body (apparently an orgasm) would occur.

While he was going through these sex motions, he would hold her pubic region and, though he wasn't trying to stimulate her, he did excite her to some degree. But then, abortively, his clutching of her genital region would come an end. He would lie talking with her a while, kiss her good night, and then go away. This happened many times during the summer. Each time, Addie was unable to sleep until hours later—she had been sexually aroused, and felt guilty about her sexual thoughts. On a few of these occasions, she masturbated herself to orgasm—and felt guilty about *that*. She was angry at her uncle for having aroused her, making her masturbate, and for never having satisfied her.

It seemed, as we went into Addie's history, she had resented all men since these sexual incidents with her uncle. Consequently, she strove to have sex relations with men that would be completely satisfying to *her*, rather than to her male partners. Although she was a nymphomaniac and had intercourse with a number of men, she managed not to satisfy a good many of them—but she would always insist that they pet her to climax. Occasionally they would be satisfied but, mostly, her sex relations consisted of heavy petting, in the course of which *she* achieved an orgasm. Then she would say she was tired or not in the mood, or she would not do her share—consequently she would leave her lover frustrated, just as she had been for those months with her uncle.

So it seemed this childhood incident was one of the main roots of Addie's nymphomania, and she easily saw and admitted this during the psychoanalysis. But she still remained compulsively promiscuous. She lost out on several males who might have made good husbands, and was getting absolutely nowhere. Addie was also still feeling guilty because she believed she should be married, not just petting. But though she understood clearly what had happened about a dozen years ago with her uncle, and realized that this was one of the main sources of her nymphomaniac tendencies, *it did her no good to see this*. When we finally broke off the psychoanalytic therapy, she had been helped in several nonsexual respects, but she was still compulsively engaging in sexual relations with men.

I felt that something was definitely wrong. I hadn't been able to help Addie to the degree that I, theoretically, could. Then, giving considerable thought to Addie's case and to several others, I began devising new methods of psychotherapy, seeking the *philosophic* basis of emotional disturbance.

I began to see that there were other reasons for Addie's problems with men and with her nymphomania. What I realized was that although I had shown her she had been hostile to her uncle, and that she still was hostile to men, I had not shown her *specifically* what she could do to rid herself of this hostility. Unless I did that, I now saw, it was unlikely she would ever give up her hostility.

I contacted Addie, told her I had thought about her case and had devised a somewhat different technique of approaching it. If she wished we would try some further sessions to see how my new ideas would work out. She said her compulsive promiscuity was about the same as it had been a year before, and that she would be willing to try a few sessions to see if she could overcome it.

This time I showed Addie that her hostility stemmed not only from the frustration her uncle had caused her, but from her *irrational attitudes* toward this frustration. She believed, as do most people, that when anyone left her frustrated, this was a horror and that her frustrator should be severely punished. She believed that anybody who did what her uncle had done to her should be blamed and chastised.

I tried to show her, first, that her uncle was not to blame for what he had done, since he hadn't meant to arouse her. He knew he was arousing *himself*, and probably believed he was getting away with it. He felt he was doing something not particularly harmful to her but helpful to him. And since she never showed any displeasure, he never had any reason to believe he had been exciting her sexually. His own knowledge of sex probably didn't allow him to realize that an eleven-year-old girl could be aroused; he hardly knew what he was doing to her when he clutched her genital region since he was completely interested in his own orgasm. But even had he known, I insisted, even had he deliberately frustrated her, at the most he would have been wrong—but he would not have been the "bastard" she thought.

"Why wouldn't he?" Addie demanded.

Because, I pointed out, he was a fallible human being, and human beings do this kind of of thing all the time. It was absolute nonsense to say, "He *shouldn't* be doing this to me!" when what she should have said was, "It would be lovely if he hadn't, but he has done it. Now what can I do to bear with his misdeed?"

Moreover, I showed Addie that because she continued telling herself, "That lousy bastard shouldn't be doing this to me," and, incensed by her own statement, she remained so preoccupied with *his* wrong-doing that *she* forgot she hadn't done anything to stop him. She hadn't even hinted that she was aroused and that he'd better stop what he was doing—or take care to satisfy her. She blamed him, saw him as a louse instead of as a mistaken human being. And until she admitted that human beings *were* continually mistaken in what they did—she would continue to be hostile.

Addie resisted accepting the fact that her uncle was not a bastard; but finally I showed her that, even if he had been aware of what he was doing, he was at worst a wrongdoer, and not terrible for *being* a wrongdoer.

She was still in contact with this uncle. Addie now began to accept him as a human being. She still didn't care for some of his behavior and was objectively critical of him. But she stopped thinking of him as a louse. Addie realized that blaming *him* was only doing *her* harm—doing nobody any good.

At the same time, I also got Addie to admit that other men, even if they acted as her uncle had, would be sad human beings, but they wouldn't be evil, terrible people. They would just be wrongdoers, and not lice for *being* wrongdoers.

As Addie started seeing this she began to be more sympathetic toward males. She stopped her sexual teasing. She had more complete sex relations—which she enjoyed. She was able to maintain longer affairs with a few men in whom she

141

was really interested, and she was no longer compulsively promiscuous in any manner. Finally, after my seeing her for eighteen sessions in the second round of psychotherapy, she was able to establish an attachment, for the first time in her life, to a single male—and she had far better sex relations with him than she had ever had.

For all practical and theoretical purposes, not only was Addie aware she had *been* hostile to her uncle years ago, and that she had unconsciously transferred this hostility to other men, but she was aware of the irrationality of her own assumptions, which made *and kept her* hostile. She was willing to admit now that it was not (*a*) her uncle's behavior that had made her angry with men for so many years, but (*b*) the nonsense she kept telling herself—namely, that he *should* not be the way he was. In this manner, Addie was able to finally overcome her compulsive promiscuity.

I tried several other cases with this new method of psychotherapy and obtained equally good results. This does not mean there is no gain from psychoanalytic treatment of nymphomaniacs; there were other compulsively promiscuous women I treated psychoanalytically who did significantly improve. In their cases, what happened was that I showed them the origin of their disturbance, how they were blaming themselves or others for something that had happened in the past and how they were transferring the past to the present. Apparently, they understood that they did not *need* to do such blaming any longer. In other words, with my indirect help, the patients said to themselves, "Well, the fact that I got upset about this thing years ago does not mean I need be upset about it now," and by their consciously or unconsciously working to change the philosophic assumption that made them and kept them upset, these patients improved.

Psychoanalysis can help at times, but I believe it is a most ineffective form of psychotherapy, especially in its classical form. At best, it reveals to people exactly what they are doing and why they are doing it, but it does not clearly reveal to them the philosophic assumptions behind what they are doing. Nor does it, in most instances, sufficiently help patients to uproot these assumptions with which they are plaguing themselves. Many psychoanalysts do approximately the same thing that I and others do in active-directive, rational-emotive, and eclectic forms of psychotherapy. They seem to do it, not on the basis of their psychoanalytic theory (which, if followed, would lead them to waste much time on childhood memories, free associations, and on analyses of transference relations), but because they are *practical psychotherapists*. It is dubious whether what these analysts do should really be called psychoanalysis, since it deviates considerably from the psychoanalytic method (Alexander and French, 1946; Berne, 1961).

Acceptiveness and permissiveness as treatment

A second method of tackling the problems of a nymphomaniac, and getting her to understand and help herself with her disturbances, is frequently the method of accepting her, i.e., being permissive and not blaming her for her activity, and through the therapeutic relationship letting her see that she is a good person despite her mistakes and that she need not keep blaming herself and remaining a nymphomaniac. Permissiveness and acceptance is frequently used by analytically-oriented psychotherapists, particularly those who follow Ferenczi (1952) and who lean over backwards to accept their patients (de Forrest, 1954; List, 1961). It's also part of the method of Rogerian or client-centered psychotherapy (Rogers, 1961). It is utilized to a considerable degree by the experientialist school in Atlanta, Ga. (Whitaker and Malone, 1953); by the existentialist therapists (Boss, 1963) and by various other schools of psychotherapy (Tarper, 1959).

Acceptance, permissiveness and unconditional positive regard can be helpful to compulsively promiscuous patients, since most nymphomaniacs, when they come for treatment, not only feel that they are self-defeating in their behavior, but that there is something bad about *them*, and *they* are to be blamed for this behavior. It is precisely this blaming of themselves for being disturbed, for being nymphomaniacs, that often interferes seriously with their overcoming the disturbance. Therapists of the client-centered, psychoanalytic and other schools who are permissive and who have a good relationship with their patient, show the patient by their behavior as well as by their words that they do not consider her evil, that they can still accept her no matter how promiscuous she may be. Theoretically, she is therefore able to accept herself.

Unfortunately, there are severe limitations to this type of therapy, for the simple reason that it does not truly contradict the underlying philosophy of the patient. The nymphomaniac who feels she is no good because she is doing badly, basically believes: "Because I am doing badly, and would be nonacceptable to others, I am worthless and should punish myself." And the therapist is saying, "No, that is not true.

Even though you are doing badly you are not worthless, because I still accept you and, therefore, you can accept yourself." But then the patient, who feels good about this, and has a boost in her so-called ego-strength, really is frequently saying to herself, "Well, my therapist accepts me, and that's nice, and shows that I'm not as bad as I think I am. But it is still true that I have to do well and be accepted by *others* to be a worthwhile human being. How do I know that other people will accept me as my therapist does?'"

This patient, then, hasn't quite given up her philosophy. In one way she is reinforcing it, having said before she went to therapy, "Because nobody accepts me, I am no good," and now saying, "Because my therapist accepts me, I am okay; I am not worthless." But she still is a dependent individual, who refuses to accept herself *whether or not* she is accepted by others. The "ego-strength" she gets is *work*-confidence or *love*-confidence (that is, she knows she can work well or have the love of others) rather than *self*-confidence. Relationship therapy may be partially effective, in the sense that it makes the patient feel better and, consequently, she may be motivated to act better. Occasionally, because she behaves relatively well (even if for the wrong reasons) she sees that she *can* really act better, that she need not be compulsively promiscuous. She may actually stop. But frequently what happens is that even though she feels better her compulsive behavior does not stop, or it stops in the *sexual* area but continues in *other* areas.

This is what I found when I used *relationship* methods, especially the Ferenczi method, which I employed for about a year with many of my patients. They did feel much better, and seemed to improve. But then, whenever I confronted them with the fact that they had to *change* their behavior, become more disciplined, and accept themselves whether or not I did, they frequently refused to work at helping themselves. In the case of one patient I saw at that time, she gave up her compulsive promiscuity as she received warmth and affection from me, and she obviously wanted me to compliment her on her improvement. I was, accordingly, quite pleased—and told her so. But unfortunately that was the only change she effected. The rest of her behavior was as disturbed as ever. She still felt terrible if anyone failed to accept her. She criticized herself mercilessly for minor failings and remained basically neurotic even though she was no longer compulsively promiscuous. This is what often takes place in relationship or acceptance therapy. The patient feels better for the moment, and believes she had increased her self-es-

144

teem. But actually she feels right for the wrong reason and is not significantly helped.

Supportive methods of treatment

Somewhat allied to relationship treatment, but more direct, is the supportive method. Here, the therapist directly and frankly tells the patient she has nothing to be guilty about, that she is a good individual, and there is no reason for her to condemn herself. Frequently, he points out her assets and tries to focus on these as well as on her presumed limitations. In one way or another he shows her that her great "crimes" are really minimal, that she can behave differently in the future. Because he supports her in this manner, the patient often feels considerably improved, and believes she has a higher estimation of herself.

But, basically, the same thing is happening here as in relationship therapy. The patient comes to believe she is not so bad because the therapist tells her she is not so bad, and because he accepts her. He shows her that although she has done these things, she has also done some *good* deeds—and he again "proves" that she is not worthless. In this form of therapy, very little, if anything, is done to change the patient's basic notions. She is shown that she does have at least one friend, the therapist, and that she does do some things well; but the implication is that if she had no friends and didn't do anything well, she would be thoroughly inadequate; and not only inadequate but a louse for being inadequate.

Here again, temporary gain is made, and this gain may be valuable. If the patient stops being a nymphomaniac because of supportive therapy, *there's a good chance she will fall back to it or to some other neurotic symptom later*, after therapy has ended, when something goes wrong in her life. I had an illustration of this in one of the cases that I worked with before I developed the theory and practice of rational-emotive psychotherapy.

SYLVIA S.

I was seeing a nineteen-year-old nymphomaniac, Sylvia S., and getting along well with her. She was terribly guilty; not only was she having sex relations with a good many males, but she was Jewish and these males were invariably non-Jewish. Her parents would have been horrified enough had they known she was having sex relations; the fact that her partners were non-Jewish would have petrified them. So,

Sylvia was blaming herself in advance, knowing how her parents would condemn her.

I tried to alleviate Sylvia's guilt by explaining, in a supportive manner, that there was something wrong with her parents for feeling the way they did. If they were going to be prejudiced because the boys with whom she went were not of their faith, then that was *their* problem. They were bigoted, and there was no reason why she had to go along with this. I showed Sylvia that her parents were mistaken and that there was nothing wrong about her behavior—except, the fact that she was compulsive. But these compulsions probably stemmed from her rebelling against the parents. The rebellion itself was not unhealthy; she was rebelling, of course, against their mistaken ideas.

So I kept supporting Sylvia and in some respects attacking her parents, because I was then more moralistic than I am today and felt that the parents were to blame for being the way they were, and it was poetic justice that Sylvia was having sex relations with precisely the men they didn't want her to know. For this reason I gave her a great deal of support. She felt wonderful at this and stopped, for a while, her compulsive promiscuity with her non-Jewish partners.

I thought things were going along well, until I discovered a few weeks later that Sylvia had started the same pattern of behavior—with Jewish partners. The support I had given her had just made her *feel* good. She was still acting essentially rebellious, even though she felt much better in some respects, and didn't consider herself a terrible person as she previously had.

By this form of supportive therapy, I had unwittingly reached *some* of Sylvia's feelings of inadequacy, her blaming herself for her symptoms, but I had not helped her to understand and eliminate her essential rebelliousness against her parents. In fact, it is possible that to some degree I had encouraged her to be rebellious, because I had shown her that her parents were wrong, and in a sense it was *right* that she should rebel. I saw later, when I was no longer in contact with this girl, that I had not reached the basis of her problem; I had not shown her that *even* though the parents were wrong, they had a right to be wrong, and she was just cutting off her nose to spite her face by rebelling against them. I was not able to see clearly, when I did this supportive therapy, that the parents *do* have a right to be wrong. I was interested in supporting the patient, even at the expense of others.

Similarly, it seems from my present vantage point, that

146

supportive treatment is at times necessary, and sometimes does some good; but it rarely gets at the philosophic basis underlying the patient's problem. It does show the patient that she is not thoroughly evil, at least in the therapist's eyes. But it doesn't show her that even if she continues to do badly, she is still not loathsome, and she can still like herself. And it does not show her how, after accepting herself by calmly accepting her errors, she can gradually learn to do better. So supportive treatment of nymphomania and of other forms of disturbance is usually a superficial form of therapy that does not get at the real root of the problem.

The rational-emotive treatment of nymphomania

I arrived at a radically different method of treating nymphomania and other forms of disturbance which I call rational-emotive psychotherapy. This method holds that while neurotic states are often originally learned by early inculcation of irrational beliefs, or by propagandization by "significant others" (such as the individual's parents), these acquired irrationalities are not automatically sustained over the years by mere lack of counter-propagandization, but they are actively re-created, reinstilled, and resuggested by the individual herself. And it is largely the individual's repeating to herself these early acquired, neurotic beliefs—rather than her parents' or others' repetitions to her—that sustain and eternally perpetuate her neurosis (Blois, 1963; Callahan, 1960; Ellis, 1962a, 1963a, 1963c; Ellis and Harper, 1961a, 1961b; Hudson, 1961; Jacobs, 1962; Lafferty, 1963; Rockberger, 1963; Wagner, 1963).

Rational-emotive therapy (RT) holds that emotions rarely have an independent existence, but are closely allied to, and are the products of, thinking. We think something is bad and we feel badly in connection with it. Or we think something is good and we feel elated about it. Most everyday thoughts are not held symbolically, pictorially, or nonverbally (as the psychoanalysts often claim), but are *verbally* represented in the individual's cognitive processes. Most emotions, as I have said, follow from simple exclamatory sentences or meanings which the individual (consciously or unconsciously) tells or signals herself immediately prior to experiencing these emotions. Neurosis, therefore, essentially consists of mistaken, illogical, and unvalidatable ideas which the individual dogmatically believes, and which she emotes—and acts upon—to her own defeat.

147

RT theory, while stating that tendencies toward irrational self-verbalizations are inborn in all human beings and agreeing that many self-defeating internal verbalizations are learned during early childhood, also insists that neurotic behavior can be acquired at any time in a person's life, particularly during her adolescent years, even if she has had an "ideal" upbringing. In regard to the emotion of anger, RT insists that, while being assertive and self-expressive, a person can definitely change and conquer rather than sublimate basic hostility. It holds that hostility invariably arises from the sane sentence, (a) "I don't like your behavior," and (b) the insane sentence, "Because I don't like your behavior, you absolutely should not display it."

The RT practioner attempts to get his patients to dispel their hostility by changing their absolutistic, grandiose sentences to: "Because I don't like your behavior, I will calmly try to induce you to change it. If I succeed, fine; but if I don't, that's all right, too. I can live successfully in a world where many people's behavior is not to my liking." Secondly, the rational therapist holds that human adults do not *need* to be accepted or loved, even though it is desirable that they be. He teaches his patients how to feel unhurt and not to be self-castigating when they are unaccepted by people who are significant to them. RT shows people how it is appropriate for them to be regretful when they are rejected, and to be frustrated or irritated when they are deprived; but it tries to teach them how to overcome all deep-seated hurt, self-depreciation and depression.

Because of its holding that human emotional disturbance is essentially ideologically and philosophically based, RT strives for a thoroughgoing philosophic reorientation of a person's outlook on life, rather than for a mere removal of psychosomatic symptoms. It tries to help the patient get rid of her general anxiety, rather than of some specific phobia, to eliminate her *generalized* tendency to hate—not only her particular hatred of her mother or husband.

There are several respects in which RT is unique as a technique of psychotherapy:

1. It is probably the only method in which the therapist tries to show the patient that she is telling herself concrete exclamatory sentences which create her disordered emotions and ineffectual behavior; and it teaches her how to observe, to logically challenge and contradict these disturbance-creating sentences. The theory of RT is that it is never the stimulus A which leads the individual to get upset at point C;

148

rather, it is *B*, what she is telling herself, usually in simple exclamatory sentences, about *A*.

2. RT is one of the most *active directed* of all psychotherapeutic methods. Its patients must not only gain insight into what nonsense they are consciously and unconsciously telling themselves, they must both think and act in counter-propagandizing ways. In RT, therefore, actual homework assignments are given: assignments such as dating a boy whom the patient is afraid to date, looking for a new job, or experimentally returning to live with a mate with whom the patient has continually quarreled. The therapist actively tries to persuade, cajole, and sometimes, command the patients to undertake such assignments as an integral part of the therapeutic process.

3. In RT, the therapist himself is usually active in therapeutic sessions, in that he does a great deal of talking. The therapist does not hesitate, even in the first session, to confront the patient directly with evidences of her irrational thinking and behavior. He very actively interprets, without worrying too much about possible resistance and defenses on the part of the patient. He consistently tries to persuade and argue the patient out of her firmly held irrational and inconsistent beliefs. And he unhesitatingly attacks the patient's neurosis-creating attitudes and ideas—after first demonstrating how and why they exist. As noted in the book, *Reason and Emotion in Psychotherapy* (Ellis, 1962a), "To the usual psychotherapeutic techniques of exploration, ventilation, excavation, and interpretation the rational therapist adds the more direct techniques of confrontation, confutation, reindoctrination and reeducation. He thereby frankly faces and resolutely tackles the most deep-seated and recalcitrant pattern of emotional disturbance."

In regard to interpretation and insight, rational therapy agrees with most neo-Freudian, Adlerian, and Jungian schools in holding that the patient's acquiring insight, especially emotional insight, into the source of her disturbance, is a most important and usually essential part of treatment. It, too, stresses interpretation as a therapeutic tool. RT, however, distinguishes between intellectual and so-called emotional insight, and operationally defines intellectual insight as the patient's knowing what is the cause of her problem and *wishing* that her knowledge would eradicate her problems, while it defines emotional insight as the patient's knowing and seeing the cause of her problems, and *working* to apply this knowledge.

RT also distinguishes three different levels of insight. *Insight No. 1* is the patient's seeing that her present neurotic behavior has antecedent causes. This is the kind of insight that is stressed by most analytic and other forms of therapy. *Insight No. 2* is the patient's acknowledging that the reason why the original causes of her disturbance *still* upset her is because she continues to believe in, and endlessly repeats to herself, the irrational beliefs that she previously acquired. *Insight No. 3* is the patient's acknowledging that there is no other way for her to get better other than by continually observing, questioning and challenging her own belief system, and by her working to change her irrational beliefs by verbal and motor counter-propagandizing activity.

RT puts relatively little emphasis on Insight No. 1, the patient's seeing the historical antecedents of her present behavior, but it particularly stresses Insights No. 2 and 3, acknowledging that *she* now keeps the original neurotic ideas alive and that *she,* and only she, can rationally-emotively think and work to eliminate them.

Rational-emotive psychotherapy overlaps in many significant ways, then, with various other schools of therapy. On theoretical grounds it has much in common with the Adlerians, the ego psychologists, the psychobiologists, the general semanticists, the directive therapists, the learning theorists and the existentialists. In regard to effecting basic personality changes in the patient, its goals and ideals are somewhat similar to those of many groups, such as the client-centered and neo-Freudian schools. Its main practices, however, are radically different in that it emphasizes rapid and forceful confrontation, a direct approach to the patient's unconscious thinking, or unverbalized attitudes, vigorous attacks on her irrational and inconsistent philosophies, homework assignments, spurs to her outside activity, energetic didactic reeducation and many other active-directive techniques which are antithetical to those employed by most therapists. It practises, moreover, are based on theoretical constructs that supplement, and in respects contradict, most therapeutic schools. In consequence, RT seems to be a distinct, new approach of therapeutic theory and practice that merits independent standing among the ever-growing variety of approaches (Harper, 1959).

In regard to the treatment of nymphomaniacs, RT particularly stresses that they must discover the basic *philosophic* assumptions on which their compulsive promiscuity rests. That is to say, they must discover the ideas and attitudes which they (usually) unconsciously hold that drive them to do what they are doing.

If the nymphomaniac will not give up these ideas, she is shown she has a right to be as sick as she wants to be and to go on believing the nonsense which makes her sick. If she is to get better, she must give up this nonsense, must accept herself as a good person in her own right whether or not other people accept her—and she must accept other people as *basically* good in their own right.

Even if, in the course of therapy, she tends to feel better, her behavior is not accepted as proof that she actually is better. Her general philosophies of life are shown to her and tackled until it looks as if she is not going to inflict herself again with similar nonsense, not drive herself into some form of obsessive-compulsive behavior other than nymphomania.

The results of treating nymphomania with the method of rational-emotive psychotherapy have been, in my practice, considerably better than the results of my previous methods of treating these compulsively promiscuous females. A study of my records shows that before I evolved the method of rational-emotive psychotherapy, I treated nine compulsively promiscuous women in either psychoanalysis or psychoanalytically-oriented therapy. In five of these cases there was significant improvement—but the women who were helped mainly became less sexually compulsive, and did not necessarily lose other symptoms which I thought equally disturbing. Since I have practiced rational-emotive psychotherapy, I have treated twenty-three females whom I would categorize as compulsively promiscuous. In twenty instances, they appeared to be significantly improved, not only in their nymphomania but in several concurrent and equally neurotic or psychotic systems. So the percentage of cure has increased distinctly, and the quality and the range of improvement has been enhanced.

Moreover, whereas the psychoanalytically treated patients were seen for an average of about ninety sessions, those patients treated with rational-emotive psychotherapy had an average range of thirty-three sessions in individual therapy, and some of them also had about thirty sessions of group therapy. So, for a fewer number of psychotherapeutic sessions over a shorter period of time, the nymphomaniacal patients treated with rational-emotive psychotherapy seemed to have done significantly better than those treated by psychoanalysis and psychoanalytic therapy.

It is to be repeated that, on the whole, women in our society who are compulsively promiscuous are usually severely disturbed individuals who are very frequently in the borderline psychotic range, rather than the neurotic phase, of disturbance. Consequently, the treatment of compulsively promiscuous women is not an easy task; it is not to be expected they will be *completely* cured, any more than other severely disturbed individuals are completely cured, in the course of intensive therapy. Nonetheless, a great deal of help can be given to these women, not only in regard to their compulsive nymphomania but also in regard to their general feelings of inadequacy and hostility.

The treatment of the compulsively promiscuous woman is by no means hopeless. It is very difficult, but it is also rewarding. When these women do settle down to their regular lives after having been successfully treated, they normally enjoy a great deal of sexual satisfaction, perhaps more than most females who never had a history of nymphomania. Along with their sexual satisfaction, they are willing to put up with a good many difficulties and disturbances of the marital state. Consequently they are able to achieve a good marital relationship.

It is much more likely that nymphomaniacs can be helped, especially in regard to their principal sex symptoms, than can other individuals (such as homosexuals, sex offenders, or other sexual deviates) who are at least equally sick—and who are not motivated to overcome their disturbances. Compulsively promiscuous women frequently are, or can be led to be, interested in overcoming their basic disturbance; considerable therapeutic hope can therefore realistically be held for them.

17

When Nymphomania
Can Be Helped

IT WILL BE USEFUL NOW, IN OUR EXAMINATION OF
nymphomania and rational-emotive therapy to review the
treatment histories of girls mentioned earlier in this book.

SUSAN

Susan's mother had reported her missing with great reluc-
tance. Although she was not overly concerned that her
daughter had been gone, the mother was horrified when she
heard the details of the sexual experience. Meeting Susan
soon after the arrest, the mother told Susan she was not sure
she wished to have her back home again. It was about this
time that Susan began to feel guilty about her sex relations.
Previously, she had gone through with them, not particularly
enjoying them, but not feeling upset.

When I spoke to Susan, before her case came to court, I
tried to show her that she had done nothing to be ashamed
of, or to feel guilty about. Even if she had made a mistake
by giving her body to men who didn't care for her, to gain
their love, this was just a mistake, and she was not to blame
for making this mistake. When I tried to reduce her guilt in
this manner, she felt better temporarily, but she was still
seriously disturbed—and not at all looking forward to returning to her mother.

Susan was put on probation and sent back to her mother,
although we at the Diagnostic Center were not happy about
this. But there was little else that could be done, except send
her to the State Home for Girls, which would perhaps be an
even greater evil.

Within a few weeks Susan had run away from home again
and had further sexual experience—with a series of males.
Once again, one of these males had brought together three of
his friends. The four of them had sex relations with Susan.
While she was having intercourse with one male, the others

153

were watching, and to some degree participating in the sex acts. Again, Susan had practically no physical pleasure except from kissing—none from actual genital contact.

Susan was deserted by one man after another as each found she had little to offer except sex. Also, the men were afraid of trouble with the police. They would leave her after a day or two, in some cases abandoning her without money or any source of help.

Despite this, Susan would continue to seek still another man. There was little doubt that this was a case of compulsive sex behavior, with Susan driven to continue her activity even though she received no sexual pleasure from it. Finally Susan was put in the reformatory for one year, because the authorities were afraid she would continue her promiscuous behavior—and become pregnant.

Characteristically enough, when she was released she resumed much the same behavior. This time she stopped running away from home; she started taking up with males in school and wherever else she could find them. Even though they had no real interest in her, she would go to bed with them.

As might be expected, her mother and father behaved worse than ever. They now considered her an absolute whore. The worse their behavior, the more Susan felt compelled to run to men. She learned to enjoy sex to a mild degree, although she was never satisfied, and could not achieve an orgasm. She never tried to focus on her own sex pleasure but only concentrated on what a great thing it was to be in a man's arms and have him accept her.

When last heard from, Susan was pursuing her self-defeating course, and was headed for almost certain psychological, if not physical, destruction. As far as is known, she has continued to be compulsively promiscuous.

Without intensive therapy, which to our knowledge she never obtained, Susan's case has a difficult but not hopeless prognosis. A few people—very few—manage to come to grips with their own situation; aided by a strong and meaningful relationship with another person who offers them love and understanding, and acceptance, they make a successful reorientation. It is highly improbable, but not impossible, that this has happened to Susan.

DOLORES

In addition to promiscuity, Dolores had another sex peculiarity: exhibitionism. Many women are moderately exhibitionistic, and carelessly dress in front of open windows. Dolores would *deliberately* do so. She was always trying to attract men with her body, and to get their interest, even when she had no intention of doing anything with them. In these cases the conquest gained was that of knowing the men did desire her, and would have gone to bed with her had she permitted it.

During her marriage, which lasted only a short while before her husband died in an accident, Dolores continued to be exhibitionistic. But, as had been the case when she lived with her parents, she behaved respectably and had only a couple of affairs during the length of her marriage. She did not wish her husband to know the type of person she was; she did not care to break up the marriage. Dolores had not married for love, but because she thought her husband a fine person who would be a good father to the children she very much desired. (She did have a child shortly after she married.) Dolores tried not to let her husband know of her sexual proclivities.

On the other hand, she was not discreet exhibitionistically. She seems to have been abetted in this to some degree by her husband, who married her, among other reasons, because she was so attractive. He was proud of the fact that when they visited friends, most of the men present paid her considerable attention. During their marriage, Dolores' conquests were mainly covetous glances of other men, but she did practically nothing about their admiration.

When her husband was killed, Dolores was sincerely distressed for several months. Left with a young child, she set about rearranging her life to support herself and her child. But about six months later, she resumed her premarital pattern of going through every man in the office where she worked, having affairs with all of them. It did not matter to her that these men were married. As long as they told her, as they often did, that she was far better—and more beautiful—then their wives, she found satisfaction. Also, she seemed to consider it a little more of a challenge to take away a man, at least temporarily, from the woman who had him, than to get a free and unattached man to go to bed with her. Dolores continued this highly promiscuous pattern for a year, and then began to get into trouble. Her activities became known, and she was fired from her job. Her girlfriends started telling her, because she was fairly open with them, that what she was doing was sick. Finally, her parents grasped what was going on, and were horrified. They came to see me, insisting that Dolores have psychotherapy. She was by then

155

willing to admit she was not having sex relations for her own pleasure, but because she compulsively needed the conquests. She admitted this was a problem to her, and she was willing to work on it in psychotherapy.

I cannot report that I quickly succeeded in showing Dolores the folly of her conquests, and in convincing her that it was pointless to get men to bed to raise her estimation of herself.

At the beginning of therapy I had a most difficult time with her. I put her, as I often do with my patients, into a therapeutic group, and although she was clearly instructed not to do so, she became personally involved with several of the males, and tried to get them into bed. We discussed these sex problems in the group and in individual therapy, but she was just recalcitrant, and I had to remove her from the group (as much for the protection of the other members of the group as of herself).

Then in individual therapy, Dolores, as might be predicted tried the same tactics with me. She indirectly and directly propositioned me, although I explained to her on more than one occasion that it is not the nature of psychotherapy, however the psychotherapist may be attracted to the patient. (This is normally counter-therapeutic, since it interferes with the process in several significant ways (Ellis, 1963g). It is also considered unethical by the psychological and therapeutic societies of which I am a member, and whose rules of ethics I follow.)

These explanations hardly stopped Dolores. She persisted and I kept showing her that she was doing to me exactly what she was doing with other men. For a long time, even though she would admit this, we got nowhere. In fact, all my efforts to convince her she was getting nothing out of the conquests were to no avail.

Then I started on a different tack. I ignored for the most part the conquests Dolores was still making (with her excuse that she really enjoyed them sexually, or that she just couldn't help herself) and tried to work on the other aspects of her disturbance. "Why," I asked, "don't you ever go after one of the few men you are truly attracted to, and try to get *him* to love you in reality, instead of just in romantic fantasies?"

Dolores was willing to admit that was one of her problems. She was worried that, if she avoided this problem, she never would be able to get along in life as she wished. We worked on this aspect of her disturbance for a while, and I kept questioning her, as I do so many of my patients, as to

156

what would be so frightful if she found a man in whom she was truly interested and if he *did* reject her, either because she had a scar on her face or for any other reason.

Dolores admitted that she could see that nothing would be so horrible. Still, the thought that she might be rejected sent cold shivers up and down her spine. She would run from any such prospect when, as occasionally happened, it did appear. So she saw the problem, and was willing to admit she was indoctrinating herself with the notion that it would be horrible, and she would be worthless, if she tried for a good man and failed. But she still did absolutely nothing about the problem. She made no effort to change this philosophy, this self-defeating attitude which she had, no matter how often I kept bringing it to her attention.

Finally, after taking a new job, Dolores found that her boss was a widower and had most of the characteristics she liked. He was intelligent, capable—and unlike most of the men with whom she went to bed. She had little interest, right from the start, in trying to conquer him. She was interested in him in other respects. Fortunately, he seemed to be quietly but steadily attracted to her, and not only physically. He respected her, and showed her in various ways that he did. Not only did he have her do his secretarial work, but he made her his hostess on occasions when he had social business affairs, and he induced her to travel on a few trips with him.

He made no attempt to establish a sexual relationship with Dolores during this time, but demonstrated that he really liked her, had a great deal of respect for her. This saved Dolores from her usual temptation to quit her job and run away from him—and to take no chances of ultimate rejection. Instead, she began slowly, with my therapeutic encouragement, to take more risks, to show him what she was really like, and to be herself when she was with him. Gradually she began to see that it might not be unbearable if, by some chance, he didn't go for her, and never wanted to marry her. Without her ever getting any dramatic insight into herself, or even working exceptionally hard to change her philosophy of life, or to challenge her own negative notion that she would be utterly worthless if her boss didn't accept her, Dolores did convince herself there was nothing so terrible about getting intensely involved. Gradually they became more committed, and finally, when they were away on a trip, they did end up in bed together—after he had told her that he liked her and would like to work things out on a more permanent basis.

This time, when she went to bed with her lover, she was

157

far from being her usually adept self. For the first time in her life, she played the role of a near-innocent, a girl who has had relatively little experience; and she was more interested in their emotional involvement with each other than with their sexual involvement.

What, fortunately, also happened was that after they had this affair and had resumed their regular routines in the city, Dolores' boss became occupied with some family affairs of his own. So they had little opportunity to get together, and she was somewhat neglected by him for the next few weeks. Although she was disturbed about this, she did work on her own feelings, and accepted that it wasn't dreadful.

She was able to acclimate herself to what almost could be called a second-class role; he was the one who was behaving neglectfully. Dolores saw she could stand on her own two feet even when the worst possible thing was happening —when the man she wanted did not seem to want her that much; and she started to gain real confidence in herself.

Dolores learned that, even when things were going badly, she did not have to be desperately unhappy. Then, with confidence born of this experience, when her boss showed interest again she was better able to risk being herself, and engage wholeheartedly in the relationship. By the time her therapy ended, she and her boss had become engaged.

Dolores did not entirely solve her problems. She still, from time to time had urges, and was tempted to do something about them. But then she reminded herself that it wasn't worth it; that she had tried promiscuity for years, and it had not given her satisfaction. It had kept her away from the intense relationship she now was achieving.

In the case of Dolores, then, although I had very little success at first in inducing her to challenge and question the *irrational* idea that she needed conquest after conquest to prove her own worth, I did finally have more success in showing her that she could take the risk of becoming involved with the kind of man she really wanted—and that she wouldn't be totally worthless if she failed to get this man.

MARJORIE L.

As true a compulsive as I have ever seen, Marjorie had to find men of a certain race or nationality, and then go on to another race, another nationality. She was frightened more by

158

the possibility that the cycle would be broken than by any of the ill effects her ritualism produced.

I pointed out to Marjorie that this form of surrender is pernicious reindoctrination. If we *believe* we should conform to a ritual, and that something dreadful will happen if we defy this rite, when we deliberately go against it, we *will* feel uncomfortable. Then, when we halt our defiance, we "feel better," because we are heeding our own belief. Every time we withdraw from a nonritualistic path and go back to the ritualistic one, we say to ourselves, "But it *would* be terrible if I didn't follow this ritual; I could not *stand* the anxiety of not going along with it." So, though it would appear that only our overt behavior is ritualistic, actually our philosophy *behind* the behavior is more important.

By the same token, if we deliberately refuse to go along with ritual—and if we tolerate the momentary anxiety—when we learn the tolerated anxiety does *not* lead to any catastrophe, we *deindoctrinate* ourselves. We subvocally note: "Well, it isn't so terrible to *not* go along with this ritual." Most of us, as in Marjorie's case, make ourselves so uncomfortable when we courageously refuse to follow our self-imposed compulsions that we quickly go back to them, and thereby indoctrinate ourselves with the notion that we *must* follow them.

This is what happened to Marjorie; she was continually reindoctrinating herself with the idea that she could not be sexual in a nonritualistic manner.

Every time I showed Marjorie this, she would agree and say, "Yes, I see that it's silly, but I just can't stop it." and I would insist, "But you can stop it. You're just indoctrinating yourself with the notion that you can't. Now, why do you continue to convince yourself, 'I can't do it,' when there's *no evidence* that you can't?"

She'd say, "Yes, but I haven't ever done it." And I'd say "Well, that's just evidence that you haven't, so far, ever given up the rituals. But that still would never prove that you *can't*. No matter how many times you have followed a silly idea, it never proves that you cannot give it up in the future. This is shown by Bowery bums who have been alcoholic for years, but who occasionally get up, go to work, and stop drinking. Other people, who have been alcoholics for twenty or thirty years, join Alcoholics Anonymous and stop drinking. Now obviously the fact that these people have been drinking for a very long time is no proof that they can't give it up. They can. As long as they *think* they can, and *work* at it, they can."

Marjorie would say, again, "Yes, I see what you mean, and I guess that you're right; but I just can't do it."

So we would quickly reach an impasse. Time after time, when I showed her that she didn't need her rituals, that they were self-defeating. She would, after some arguing, finally agree; but she still wouldn't give them up. Then, when I would get her to give up certain things, some of her food and washing compulsions, she acquired substitute rituals. She made little headway against her general compulsive behavior pattern.

I could see that even if I were successful in getting her to give up this or that compulsion, it would take forever before she would really stop being a compulsive. Moreover, she could easily add new compulsions. I realized that in her case, as in most such cases, I would have to get to the core of the matter, to show her that it was her general quest for certainty which was self-destructively driving her.

I tried to convince Marjorie that since she had compulsions from the earliest days she could remember (when she was three or four years old) and since these rituals went on without allaying her anxiety, obviously she still followed them because she had a general need for certainty. She kept telling herself she couldn't exist in this world of probability and chance, and that for somebody who was as inadequate and worthless as she, there had to be inflexible, invariant rules of behavior by which she could guide herself.

At first, she would not even admit she believed herself inadequate. When she was able to keep up with some of the rituals for awhile, she felt quite good. Thereby she "proved" to herself she was self-disciplined. I showed her this was false reasoning. The fact that she *had* to continue the ritual, was *compelled* to do so, and felt *so good* after this self-discipline, showed that underneath she really didn't like herself. If anything, it was a negative, needless thing to do; she was patting herself on the back for her ritualistic handwashings and food rigidities, saying how good she was when, clearly, she was protesting too much, displaying her underlying insecurity.

It took a little while, but I finally showed Marjorie that her surface superiority feelings were a mask for her severe inadequacy feelings, which were just below this surface. She was willing to admit, when I confronted her with other manifestations of her anxiety, that after she successfully accomplished her ritualistic feats she tended to become depressed and she had to pull out of her hat still another form

160

of compulsive behavior to *prop herself up* again. In other words, she was always falling down, feeling depressed; then she would pull herself up by ritualistic behavior. She then, temporarily, would feel elated, almost manic; then, bingo! she would start falling back and have to do the whole thing over again. The fact that she had to continually repeat the compulsive process proved that she had strong feelings of inadequacy underneath, for which she had to keep compensating. Finally Marjorie was able to admit this.

I was then able to relate these acts to her *perfectionist* demands. She felt inadequate because she demanded of herself that she be perfect. Her rituals and compulsions incorporated her demands for perfect order. She could not afford to have anything (such as her food, handwashings, or housecleaning) in disarray, because then she would not be the "greatest of the great." If she kept *everything* in order, then she would be better than anyone else.

Marjorie's basic philosophy, was: "If I am not at the top of the list at practically everything I undertake, then I am no good *at all;* I am utterly worthless." But, instead of curling up and dying when she got into one of her frequent depressed states, she *did* have the courage, one might say, to fight again, and so pull herself up by the taxing technique of ritualistic compulsive behavior.

I insisted that she did feel worthless underneath, that her inadequacy was largely a function of her perfectionistic demands on herself. The *only way* that she could get to feel less inadequate was to give up some of these demands and to accept herself as a human being—who makes mistakes. Even when a person was more competent than other people (which Marjorie was, in several respects), she could never be infallible.

We plugged away on this line. I showed Marjorie, time and again, that it wasn't awful to make mistakes, that she could accept herself as a mistake-maker, and that she need not consider herself horrible because she was fallible and did commit errors. Again Marjorie resisted and resisted. She would agree in an intellectual way with me, and say, *yes* she saw that what I was saying was correct. But then she would not work at being the unguilty (if still fallible) person we were trying to get her to be. On the contrary, she would quickly go back to her rituals.

The perniciousness of ritualistic symptoms such as these is that one works so hard at constructing and maintaining them that one has little time to work on oneself to change the basic philosophic viewpoints which induce the symptoms. So another vicious circle is created.

By degrees Marjorie was able to accept herself as fallible, as imperfect, and not demand ideal performance of herself. At the same time I was chipping away at her perfectionism, I was showing her that she *had* to give up her notion of certainty, and *had* to accept the idea that the universe is based on probability and chance; if she did not do so she was bound to destroy herself. Time after time, as she could see, there was no certainty. She would plan something, and then see it could not succeed. Then she'd get terribly upset. I kept pointing out to her that if she demanded certainty, and if the facts of life showed that she wouldn't get it, what could happen other than her getting upset? Anxiety basically consists of: (*a*) demanding that something be a certain way, then seeing at (*b*) that it is not going to be that way, and then at (*c*) feeling uncomfortable, panicked.

Another way of putting this to say that if people *ask* things from life, and are disappointed, they can end up by saying, "Well, too bad I didn't get what I wanted." But if they *demand*, and their demands are unfulfilled, they can only end up by saying, "My God, I'm not going to get my demand; I can't stand being without it, and I've got to collapse!" That's what Marjorie was doing. The quest for certainty, I insisted, could only lead to continued anxiety.

Whenever Marjorie came to see me, panic-stricken, I was able to show her once again she was demanding something, was not getting what she demanded (because life just isn't that way), and then, because she had unrealistic demands, she was making herself anxious.

This happened on one occasion in regard to her sex compulsivity. After she had gone with an Italian, then with a Greek, then with a mid-western American, and now was prepared to go with a Negro—another Greek turned up. The The boy really attracted Majorie. He was interested in her, and she would have enjoyed having an affair with him. But he didn't fit into her compulsive pattern.

I showed her that she *had* to be disturbed, as a result of her own definitions. Here, once again, life was not going according to the order which she demanded of it, and therefore she was, inevitably, upset. Then, I returned to the basic reasons for Marjorie's unrealistic demands. Why, I asked her, did her sex affairs have to be in this order, or for that matter, in any order? She couldn't give me any reason, except to say she felt more comfortable when it was in the

162

"right" order. I replied, "That's because you *insist* that only that procedure feels comfortable. Just as an Orthodox Jew insists he cannot eat pork because it would make him uncomfortable and then becomes uncomfortable when he does eat the pork, you're insisting that the next boy be a Negro (when you actually want a Greek) and are thereby *creating* your own discomfort."

Marjorie said, "But if I take up with this Greek boy, and go against the way I usually do things, then I'm sure it won't turn our right."

"What makes you so sure?" I asked. "Do you mean that fate would punish you for not following your preordained pattern of going with men?"

"I guess that's what I do feel, that fate will punish me for going against it."

"But there is no fate, that idea is pure magic. You say that you are not a believer in the Catholic faith in which you were raised, that you have no particular religion. But you *do* have a religion, a religion of 'fate.' This is one of the silliest of all magical beliefs. Obviously, your particular concept of fate can't be true, since most other girls don't follow the dating patterns that you insist are necessary or fated, and somehow or other they are not doomed. Isn't that so?"

"Yes, I guess I get into more difficulty with men than other girls do."

So I said: "If there is any fate, then, it seems to be a fate which is purely designed for you, and not for the other people in the world."

"I never thought of that before."

"Maybe you'd better think of it."

She thought for awhile and said, "Yes, I guess it is special, for me."

"That's exactly the point," I emphasized. "You are *especially* making up, fabricating, creating this silly fate; and then you are doggedly sticking to it."

"But why do I have to make this up?"

"Only because you think you must; because you think you cannot go out and enjoy yourself in this probabilistic universe and take the chance that things will work out all right. You insist they've got to work out perfectly; and the only way you can think of insuring this is to invent an imaginary fate, as you have done, and to try and force the disparate events in the universe into a 'fated' pattern."

This really shook Marjorie up. She began to see that she herself was creating the fate which, peculiarly enough, was supposed to rule the whole universe. And this fate didn't in

163

the least rule the universe; it ruled her. But it only ruled her because she created it, and because she insisted that it did. She also began to see that she would be better off, without this fate; it was, in other words, completely superfluous; it only existed by her own unverifiable definitions; and she was most unhappy when she went against it because she defined herself as necessarily unhappy when she defied it. So the whole thing was a pure fabrication.

Then, when I had begun to make some inroads in showing Marjorie that the fate she had imagined for the universe, and really for herself, was fabricated in regard to her sexual affairs, I went on to show her that her cleansing, food, and other rituals were similarly fate-oriented. For, again, practically everybody else in the world ate vegetables in a supposedly chaotic order and they obviously weren't dropping dead all around, while she was having more pain and trouble sticking compulsively to her schedule than they were having. Yet she was insisting that she *must* eat that way.

I kept showing her, with more examples, that it was always the same pattern; she couldn't accept any disorder in the universe, and felt obliged to create an artificial order. This perfectionistic philosophy was mainly a *vote of nonconfidence in herself*, which practically all neurotic and psychotic symptoms are.

Marjorie became disturbed at this revelation that she was really weak, and that she was trying to build pseudo-strength by her rigid compulsions. She became so upset, in fact, that she started to blame herself for having the type of weakening symptom she had. But I soon stopped her from going down *that* path.

Practitioners of rational-emotive psychotherapy just don't show patients what they are doing to themselves and then let them berate themselves for doing it. We show them that whatever they are doing to themselves, and whatever their symptoms may be, they are not to blame for their misdeeds. They are disturbed human beings who act badly, who defeat their own ends, but they are not, nor can they be, *evil* for being disturbed. Self-ascribed evil is a moralistic, metaphysical concept which humans neurotically add.

In other words, in rational-emotive psychotherapy, the worst an individual can be is ineffective. When she is ineffective, she is not doing the correct thing, which she would like to do herself, nor creating a world in which she would like to live. But she is not "a louse" for *being* ineffective. She is merely a mistaken human who, if she accepts herself as a wrongdoer (but *not* a sinner!), can work and practice, think and act,

164

until finally she becomes less inefficient and more efficient. But she *never* will be utterly efficient.

So, as Marjorie started to blame herself for being inefficient, I showed her that she was taking a sane sentence, "I now see that I'm doing badly and defeating my own ends; this is sad, this is deplorable, this is bad," and adding the insane sentence, "Because I am doing badly, I am worthless and I could never possibly do well again in the future."

The latter is a wholly unprovable, metaphysical sentence because there is no evidence that a human being who has done badly for a long time and still is, cannot possibly do better again. There can only be evidence that *so far* she has not done well. Presumably she may, by work and thinking and practice, be able to do better in the future. And even if she never does better, that still doesn't prove that she is a worthless *person*.

Gradually, I was able to build up Marjorie's estimation of herself by showing her that her negative feelings, which had been masked to a large degree by her compulsive activities, were illegitimate and definitional, and they could not be scientifically sustained. She looked at these negative feelings and thought about them and saw that they were unsustainable—and she began to accept herself with her human fallibilities.

Once this significant inroad against her self-defeating philosophies of life was achieved, I broadened it to show Marjorie that in *no* respect was it necessary to blame herself, nor to insist she must live in a perfect world and be a perfect human being. I continued tackling her demands, her needs for certainty, showing her they need not exist. It might be fine if she were perfect, I agreed. But what was desirable was not necessary.

As Marjorie's demands for certainty started to wane, several symptoms began to fade. The nymphomania, in which she compulsively went with one man after another, was one of the last symptoms to go, perhaps because it was giving her distinct neurotic gains. But some of the other symptoms diminished, and then finally started to disintegrate.

There was a specific help in cracking Marjorie's compulsive promiscuity when I was able to show her that one of the reasons she changed men so rapidly was the underlying fear that they would discover her compulsiveness and her sickness. Even though she pretended on the surface, before she went to therapy, that her compulsions were indications of superiority, she knew perfectly well that others would think them peculiar. Her actual nymphomania, or running from one man to another, was motivated by not wanting to be found out by each one.

As her symptoms started to decrease, and as I showed her she was never to blame for being the way she was, and that it was not a shameful thing if somebody found out she was emotionally disturbed, she started to change partners on a more realistic basis.

PART FIVE

Maturity

18

Today's Sexually Liberated Female

WHAT DOES IT ALL ADD UP TO? WHAT CAN BE DONE about the problem of nymphomania? In this book, we have seen the nymphomaniac as a sick person, who engages in sexual activites for the wrong reasons and in self-defeating ways. It is not sexual pleasure that makes her sick; it is, rather, *not* having such pleasure. Activity, yes; enjoyment, no.

We have closely observed the nymphomaniac and have indicated some of the reasons she engages in irrational, unenjoyable, repetitive and uncontrollable behavior: her restrictive beliefs, youthful rebellion, and frantic search for love caused by the fear that she is unlovable; her need for conquest and power, and so on. We must be careful to include however, that *many—indeed, most—girls with similar neurotic motives do not became nymphomaniacs*. Some may become frigid; others, compulsive careerists; while still others may develop neurotic trends that manifest themselves in different ways. But if the disturbance takes a form of deviant sexuality, whether they become lesbians, nymphomaniacs or anything else, they become objects of scorn in our society. To their original difficulties, there is *added* a new one: a lowered self-image because society tells them they are degenerate, rather than sick—*because they accept society's estimate* of themselves and make it their own.

We must, therefore, approach the subject of preventing and curing compulsive female promiscuity in two ways: First, we must make an effort to isolate those factors in the social organism that encourage this type of neurosis or psychosis. Such knowledge can lead to therapeutic changes, because it *is* possible for families to escape the traps set for them by society. Even in a sick culture, families may rear emotionally healthy children—although it is more difficult for them to do so. Knowledge of those social factors which encourage nymphomania can help in the gradual alteration of the rigid social attitudes that encourage unhealthy sexual concepts.

Secondly, where preventing nymphomania fails, as it must in some instances, help can be given in various ways. (*a*) The nymphomaniac can be treated by psychotherapy, which we belive is best conducted by modern active-directive methods, and not through lengthy, time-consuming soul-searching. (*b*) She can be helped through an accepting, nonblaming, understanding attitude by those with whom she has contact, in which she is seen as an ailing but worthwhile person.

It would be amiss to close this book without saying something about the *healthy* highly-sexed woman, who should never be confused with the compulsively promiscuous female.

Woman as a sexual being is only beginning to come into her own in America and in other parts of the Western world. The male in our society is expected to sow his wild oats; the woman who does this still essentially regarded as a tramp. The male who, at the age of twenty-two or thereabouts, is a virgin is made ashamed of this status; the woman is ashamed of any other. The man is expected to find sexual satisfactions wherever he can (as long as it is heterosexual)—and society offers admiration and encouragement, although occasionally he is frowned upon if his activities become outrageous to the public. But a woman who copulates because she enjoys it is scorned by many respectable people.

We have come a way—not a long way—from the time when woman was looked upon as sexless (when sex was thought dirty, and woman pure). The concept of the "pure" woman is still with us; the female is allowed interest in sex, provided it is monogamous and ultraromantic.

But what has happened to the women's rights movement? What has happened to woman's struggle for equality? Can there by any equality between the sexes if the male is a hero when he indulges in considerable sexual activities without love, and when the woman doing the same thing is condemned as a whore—or a "nymphomaniac." "She's a pushover," a man will say, in contempt—and then he chases her in the hope that it is true. But when he says, "She's a pushover," it is rare to find the man who will ask *himself*: "Aren't you?" Or ask himself: "If it is so abhorrent for her to behave in this manner, why is it not equally so for you?"

This double standard of morality is rooted in history, in religion, in the family, in economics, but we need not go into its genesis at this point. It is sufficient to note that it exists. A generation ago, there was a good deal of talk about the double standard. Today, the expression is heard infrequently, but the concept is still with us. If there has been some relaxation in its rigidity, the basic attitudes are nonetheless present, as they were when Ibsen's Nora, almost a century ago, cried out in anguish against a system that gave sexual freedom to men but not to women (Friedan, 1962).

Many men proclaim they would like to see women sexually awakened and free to indulge in behavior which today brings forth great condemnation. But what they really mean is that they would like to see more loose women around for them to exploit. The men often want to use these women —and then discard them. They would not see these women as fit wives. They do not want the double standard relaxed; they actually seek to have it reinforced.

This double standard means: (*a*) that it is quite acceptable to be a sexually promiscuous male, but an equally promiscuous female is *ipso facto* disrespectable and most indecent; and this in turn requires: (*b*) that women are in two groups, the good and the bad, or those who do and those who don't. And although we are at this moment concerning ourselves with the nefarious effect of this hypocritical standard on the development of the sexually awakened woman, let it be said, as an aside, that the double standard *has a disastrous effect on the males as well.* For the two classes of women are supposed to be available to our young men: the good to be loved, but not touched; and the bad to be touched, but not loved. Then comes marriage, and the young man is suddenly supposed to be able to make a great transformation, and combine sex-and-love and love-and-marriage.

But what does this do to the healthy female? It leaves her little room, if she is going to internalize the attitudes of those in her society, to consider herself worthwhile, and still to engage in a free, happy, controlled, noncompulsive sexual life. She is the type of woman who enjoys sex, but is not driven to it; she can integrate it into her life, rather than allow it to rule her life. But if she has more than one lover at a time—as George Sand, Rey Anthony, and other healthy women mentioned in this book evidently have had—she is called promiscuous—by men who are themselves leading far more promiscuous lives than she is ever likely to lead.

Can a noncompulsive promiscuous woman have a high opinion of herself? One noted psychoanalyst (Reik, 1963) thinks not:

> Whatever the deeper motives are for a woman's promiscuity, her behavior is inevitably accompanied by a loss of self-esteem and results in contempt for herself as an individual and for her sex. It corrupts her self-image when she is degraded to the position of a sexual object of the male. No woman with a high opinion of herself as a person and as a member of her sex will drift into promiscuity except in utter despair or under the pressure of dire need of money. The demoralizing effect of promiscuity is akin to that of a woman who sells herself into slavery.

If one omits the moralistic word "promiscuity," and substitutes for it such an unemotional term as "varietism" of "sexual varietism," then Reik's statement, although somewhat accurate, shows how far our society is circular in a defeatist and rather vicious manner. For, first, the society defines the girl who is sexually active and varietist as degraded, and then (after imposing this view on the girl herself) condemns her behavior "inevitably accompanied by a loss of self-esteem" —which is precisely what the degradation is supposed to consist of!

But why is female sex varietism accompanied by this loss of self-esteem? And we mean her normal, healthy, *varietist* sex, indulged in for pleasure—usually far less promiscuously, more romantically, and certainly more discriminatively than often characterized male varietism. Why does a sexually active woman see herself as degraded?

170

It was a major contention of George Herbert Mead and many others (Mead, 1936; Cooley, 1902; Sullivan, 1947) that people see themselves as mirror images of how they *believe* they appear to the world around them. Hence, according to this theory, if women believe their boyfriends, co-workers, brothers or mothers see them as degraded and degenerate, or would thus evaluate them if they knew the truth about what they did in bed last night, these women will accept this view of themselves, and hence there will be an inevitable—or an almost but not quite inevitable—loss of self-esteem.

But here two factors enter, which Mead ignored, and to which Reik and most others pay little attention: First, cultural attitudes are not necessarily good or correct from a mental hygiene standpoint, and should be subjected to constant questioning to determine their inherent irrationalities and contradictions, so the individual can discover whether the attitudes imposed on him should themselves be changed. And, second, it is true the *most* of us *usually* accept the views we think are held by the world around us (which Mead termed "the generalized other") and, particularly, by the meaningful people in our lives (whom Mead called "the significant others,") but it is hardly necessary—and certainly not inevitable—to internalize and accept *every* view of ourselves that we believe the world may have. In fact, it would be a sorry universe of conformity and self-condemnation if each of us were so other-directed—to use the term that has been hammered away at in recent years (Fromm, 1962; Riesman, 1953)—and if we thought, acted and reacted exactly as we believe our peer groups expect us to think, act, and react.

If society, then, is driving the promiscuous woman into the despair of self-contempt, it may be more useful, both for her and her social group, to work at diminishing her self-contempt, rather than focus on reducing her promiscuity. But this would involve *re-evaluating woman as a sexual being*; it would mean *accepting* her as such.

A few women seem to reject social condemnation, and hold high self-esteem while asserting their rights to a free sex life. For these women, one writer (Hirsch, 1963) utilizes the phrase, "the love elite." A woman who belongs to this group, Hirsch contends, understands that she is free; and the love elite woman is capable of accepting responsibility with freedom. She makes her own distinction between the rational and irrational demands of society.

In love and sexual relationships she demands to be free. She has asserted her equality with the man—has rejected once and for all an inferior "second sex" status. She accepts no authority determining her use of her body or mind. Her affections and her intimacies henceforth will be freely bestowed—or not bestowed at all.

Thus, she is sometimes at odds with society's values—values still based upon a time when woman was subordinate. Because she has gone beyond society's values—truly risen above them—her "indiscretions" may lead her into difficulties. But if difficulties arise, they are less catastrophic because she knows, or believes that the values of society—not her own—are at fault.

There are, of course, biological as well as social reasons, as the French writer (de Beauvoir, 1953) points out, for the erotic life of woman to be different from that of man. But there is no biological reason why, for a woman who freely chooses a nonmonogamous life, ostracism should be inflicted upon her by men who themselves are transgressors—and who encourage and assist her in every way to violate the restrictive, established codes.

While we have devoted the greater part of this book to a study of those women who are disapproved of for expressing their sexuality in a sick compulsive manner, there are large numbers of women equally condemned by society for pursuing sex lives that are controlled, healthy, and free. In their cases, it is the *definition* of their activities as evil that creates internal difficulties for them; or, rather, it is their capitulation to the pressure to accept these negative, antifemale judgments.

America and the Western world must still make long strides toward the emancipation of women. Such emancipation will not exist until a female has the right to choose to have lovers as a man so chooses, and until she lives in a group that does not inflict upon her the notion that she is a fallen women when she loves freely.

A few women suffer from nymphomania or compulsive promiscuity. But many, many more suffer from lack of sexual freedom, from condemnation of their free lives, and from

172

pressures to survive and retain a healthy self-image in an unegalitarian atmosphere. When sexually alive women are full accepted, and are not considered over-sexed trollops, much of the anguish will be relieved. This will be a great stride toward implementing the progress made in the last century in regard to economic and political liberation of woman.

References

Alexander, Franz, and French, Thomas M. *Psychoanalytic therapy*. New York: Ronald, 1946.

Allen, Clifford. *The sexual perversions and abnormalities*. London: Oxford, 1949.

Allen, Clifford. Nymphomania. *Sexology*, Sept. 1962.

Allen, Clifford, *et al. The adrenal cortex and intersexuality*. London: Chapman and Hall, 1938.

Anthony, Rey. *The housewife's handbook on selective promiscuity*. Tucson, Ariz.: Seymour Press, 1960; New York: Documentary Books, 1962.

Atwater, Richard. *See* Procopius.

Beauvoir, Simone de. *The second sex*. New York: Knopf, 1953.

Benjamin, Harry. Prostitution. In Ellis, Albert, and Abarbanel, Albert (Eds.). *The encyclopedia of sexual behavior*. New York: Hawthorn Books, 1961.

Benjamin, Harry, and Masters R. E. L. *Prostitution and morality*. New York: Julian Press, 1964.

Berne, Eric. *Transactional analysis in psychotherapy*. New York: Grove Press, 1961.

Bloch, Iwan. *The sexual life of our time*. London: Rebman, 1908.

Blois, R. S. Dr. Ellis: a comparison of rational therapy and the structural differential. *Symbols*, 1963, Oct.-Nov. 1963, 3-4.

Boss, Medard. *Daseianalysis*. New York: Basic Books, 1963.

Brittain, A. *Roman women*. Philadelphia, 1907.

Bromley, Dorothy D., and Britten, F. H. *Youth and sex*. New York: Harper, 1938.

Brown, Helen Gurley. *Sex and the single girl*. New York: Bernard Geis, 1962.

Callahan, Roger J. Value orientation and psychotherapy. *Amer. Psychologist,* 1960, 15, 269-270.

Clark, Le Mon. Sexual adjustment in marriage. In Ellis, Albert, and Abarbanel, Albert (Eds.). *The encyclopedia of sexual behavior*. New York: Hawthorn Books, 1961.

Cooley, Charles Horton. *Human nature and the social order*. New York: Scribner's, 1902.

Cory, Donald Webster. *The homosexual in America*. New York: Paperback Library, 1963.

174

Cory, Donald Webster. *The lesbian in America.* New York. Citadel Press, 1964.

Davis, Katharine B. *Factors in the sex life of twenty-two hundred women.* New York: Harper, 1929.

Davis, Kingsley. The sociology of prostitution. *Amer. Sociol. Rev.,* 1937, 2, 744-755.

De Forrest, Izette. *The leaven of love.* New York: Harper, 1954.

Delgado, José M. R. Control of behavior by electronic stimulation of the brain. *Naval Research* Reviews; quoted by Robert Coughlan. Behavior by electronics. *Life,* Mar. 8, 1963.

De Ropp, Robert S. *Drugs and the mind.* New York: St. Martin's, 1957.

Diaz-Guerrera, Rogelio. Socratic therapy. In Standal, Stanley W., and Corsini, Raymond J. (Eds.). *Critical incidents in psychotherapy.* Englewood Cliffs, N. J.: Prentice-Hall, 1959.

Dio Cassius. *History of Rome.* Troy, N. Y., 1905.

Drugs influencing sexual desire and performance. *Medical letter on drugs and therapeutics,* June 7, 1963, 5, 45-46.

Dubois, Paul. *The psychic treatment of nervous disorders.* New York: Funk and Wagnalls, 1907.

Durant, Will. *Caesar and Christ.* New York: Simon and Schuster, 1944.

Ellis, Albert. *How to live with a neurotic.* New York: Crown Publishers, 1957.

Ellis, Albert. *The art and science of love.* New York: Lyle Stuart, 1960.

Ellis, Albert. *The folklore of sex.* New York: Grove Press, 1961.

Ellis, Albert. *Reason and emotion in psychotherapy.* New York: Lyle Stuart, 1962b.

Ellis, Albert. Rational-emotive psychotherapy. Paper read at the American Psychological Association convention, St. Louis, August 31, 1962b.

Ellis, Albert. *If this be sexual heresy* ... New York: Lyle Stuart, 1963a.

Ellis, Albert. *The intelligent woman's guide to man-hunting.* New York: Lyle Stuart, 1963c.

Ellis, Albert. *The origin and development of the incest taboo.* Published with Durkheim, Emile. *Incest: the taboo and its origin.* New York: Lyle Stuart, 1963c.

Ellis, Albert. *The American sexual tragedy.* New York: Lyle Stuart, 1962; New York: Grove Press, 1963d.

Ellis, Albert. *Sex and the single man.* New York: Lyle Stuart, 1963e.

Ellis, Albert. Constitutional factors in homosexuality. In Belgel, Hugo, G. (Ed.). *Advances in sex research.* New York: Hoeber-Harper and Row, 1963f.

Ellis, Albert. To thine own therapeutic lust be true??? Paper read at the American Psychological Association convention, August 31, 1963g.

Ellis, Albert. *The theory and practice of rational-emotive psychotherapy.* New York: Lyle Stuart, 1964.

Ellis, Albert, and Abarbanel, Albert (Eds.). *The encyclopedia of sexual behavior*. New York: Hawthorn Books, 1961.

Ellis, Albert, and Harper, Robert A. *A guide to rational living*. New York: Prentice-Hall, 1961a.

Ellis, Albert, and Harper, Robert A. *Creative marriage*. New York: Lyle Stuart, 1961b.

Ellis, Havelock. *Studies in the psychology of sex*. New York: Random House, 1936.

Feré, Charles Samson: *Scientific and esoteric studies in sexual degeneration in mankind and in animals*. New York: Anthropological Press, 1932.

Ferenczi, Sandor. *Further contributions to the theory and technique of psychoanalysis*. New York: Basic Books, 1952.

Finch, Bernard. *Passport to paradise . . . ?* New York: Philosophical Library, 1960.

Freud, Sigmund. *Collected papers*. 5 vols. New York: Basic Books, 1955.

Friedan, Betty. *The feminine mystique*. New York: Norton, 1962.

Fromm, Erich. *The art of loving*. New York: Harper Colophon, 1962.

Greenwald, Harold. *The call girl: a social and psychoanalytic study*. New York: Ballantine Books, 1958.

Grimes, Pierre. Alcibiades. A dialogue using the dialectic as a mode of psychotherapy for alcoholics. *Quart. J. Studies Alc.*, 1961, 22, 277-297.

Hamilton, G. V. *A research in marriage*. New York: Boni, 1929.

Harper, Robert A. *Psychoanalysis and psychotherapy: thirty-six systems*. Englewood Cliffs, N. J.: Prentice-Hall, 1959.

Hartman, Robert: *The measurement of value*. Crotonville, N. Y.: General Electric Co., 1959.

Hartman, Robert. *The individual in management*. Chicago: Nationwide Insurance Co., 1961.

Heard, Gerald. Can this drug enlarge man's mind? *Psychedelic Review*, Summer 1963, p. 7.

Henriques, Fernando: *Prostitution and society*. New York: Citadel Press, 1963.

Hesse, Erich. *Narcotics and drug addiction*. New York: Philosophical Library, 1946.

Hirsch, Arthur H. *The love elite*. New York: Julian Press, 1963.

Hirsch, Edwin W. *Modern sex life*. New York: New American Library, 1957.

Hirschfeld, Magnus. *Sexual anomalies: the origins, nature, and treatment of sexual disorders*. New York: Emerson Books, 1948.

Hudson, John. *Values and psychotherapy*. In manuscript, 1961.

Hühner, Max. *A practical treatise on disorders of the sexual function in the male and female*. Philadelphia: F. A. Davis, 1916.

Huxley, Aldous. *The devils of London*. New York: Harper, 1952.

Jacobs, Gordon. A new approach to psychotherapy. Talk delivered to the Morristown Unitarian Fellowship, Dec. 9, 1962.

Johnson, Virginia E., and Masters, William H. Intravaginal contraceptive study. Phase I. Anatomy. *West. J. Surg. Obstet. & Gynecol.*, 1962, 70, 202-207.

Karpman, Benjamin. *The sexual offender and his offenses.* New York: Julian Press, 1954.

Kelly, G. Lombard. Menopause. In Ellis, Albert, and Abarbanel, Albert (Eds.). *The encyclopedia of sexual behavior.* New York: Hawthorn Books, 1961.

Kinsey, A. C., Pomeroy, W. B., and Martin, C. E. *Sexual behavior in the human male.* Philadelphia: Saunders, 1948.

Kinsey, A. C., Pomeroy, W. B. Martin, C. E., and Gebhard, P. H. *Sexual behavior in the human female.* Philadelphia: Saunders, 1953.

Kirkendall, Lester A. Sex drive. In Ellis, Albert and Abarbanel, Albert (Eds.). *The encyclopedia of sexual behavior.* New York: Hawthorn Books, 1961.

Krafft-Ebing, R. v. *Psychopathia sexualis.* Brooklyn, N. Y.: Physicians and Surgeons Book Co., 1922 (original English edition, 1906; original German edition, 1886).

Kupperman, Herbert S. Sex hormones. In Ellis, Albert, and Abarbanel, Albert (Eds.). *The encyclopedia of sexual behavior.* New York: Hawthorn Books, 1961.

Lafferty, J. Clayton. *Values that defeat learning.* In manuscript, 1963.

List, Jacob S. *Education for living.* New York: Philosophical Library, 1961.

Lolli, Giorgio. *Social drinking: the effects of alcohol.* New York: Collier Books, 1961.

Lombroso, Cesare: *Crime, its causes and remedies.* Boston: Little, Brown, 1918.

London, Louis S. *Sexual deviations in the female.* New York: Julian Press, 1957*a*.

London, Louis S. *Abnormal sexual behavior.* New York: Julian Press, 1957*b*.

MacDougald, Duncan, Jr. Aphrodisiac. In *Encyclopedia Britannica.* Chicago: University of Chicago Press, 1955.

MacDougald, Duncan, Jr. Aphrodisiacs and anaphrodisiacs. In Ellis, Albert, and Abarbanel, Albert (Eds.). *The encyclopedia of sexual behavior.* New York: Hawthorn Books, 1961.

Mann, Thomas. *Joseph in Egypt.* New York: Knopf, 1938.

Masters, R. E. L. *Eros and evil.* New York: Julian Press, 1962*a*.

Masters, R. E. L. *Forbidden sexual behavior and morality.* New York: Julian Press, 1962*b*.

Masters, R. E. L. and Lea, Eduard. *Sex crimes in history.* New York: Julian Press, 1963.

Masters, William H., and Johnson, Virginia. Anatomy of the female orgasm. In Ellis, Albert, and Abarbanel, Albert (Eds.). *The encyclopedia of sexual behavior.* New York: Hawthorn Books, 1961.

Masters, William H., and Johnson, Virginia E. The sexual response cycle of the human female. III. The clitoris: anatomic and clinical considerations. *West. J. Obstet. & Gynecol.*, 1962, 270, 248-257.

Mead, George Herbert. *Mind, self and society.* Chicago: University of Chicago Press, 1936.

Michelet, Jules. *Satanism and witchcraft: a study in medieval superstition.* New York: Walden, 1939.

Oleck, Jack. *Messalina.* New York: Lyle Stuart, 1959.

Oliven, John F. *Sexual hygiene and pathology.* Philadelphia: Lippincott, 1955.

Phillips, E. Lakin: *Psychotherapy.* Englewood Cliffs, N. J.: Prentice-Hall, 1956.

Procopius. *Secret history.* Translated from the Greek by Richard Atwater. New York: Covici-Friede, 1934.

Real Life Guide. Note preceding "Marriage to a nymphomaniac," by Harry F. Tashman, Nov. 1962.

Reik, Theodor. *The need to be loved.* New York: Farrar, Straus, 1963.

Riesman, David, with Glazer, Nathan, and Denney, Reuel. *The lonely crowd.* New York: Doubleday (Anchor Books), 1953.

Rockberger, Harry. Rational-emotive psychotherapy: a few comments. *Bull. Essex Country Soc. Clin. Psychologists in Priv. Practice,* March 1963, 6, No. 1, 5-6.

Rogers, Carl R. *On becoming a person.* Boston: Houghton Mifflin, 1961.

Shiff, Nathan A. *Diary of a nymph.* New York: Lyle Stuart, 1961.

Shuttleworth, Frank. A biosocial and developmental theory of male and female sexuality. *Marr. Fam. Living,* 1959, 21, 163-170.

Suetonius. *Works.* Cambridge: Harvard University Press, 1939.

Sullivan, Harry Stack. *Conceptions of modern psychiatry.* Washington: Wm. Alanson White Foundation, 1947.

Sullivan, Harry Stack. *The interpersonal theory of psychiatry.* New York: Norton, 1953.

Thorne, Frederick C. Personality: a clinical eclectic view. Brandon, Vermont: *Journal of Clinical Psychology,* 1961.

Tillich, Paul. *The courage to be.* New York: Oxford University Press, 1953.

Wagner, Edwin E. Techniques of rational counseling. *High Spots,* 1963, 3, No. 6, 2.

Whitaker, Carl A., and Malone, Thomas A. *Roots of psychotherapy.* New York: McGraw-Hill, 1953.

Woodward, L. T. *Sex and hypnosis.* Derby, Conn.: Monarch Books, 1961.

Woodward, L. T. *The deceivers.* New York: Universal Publishing (Beacon-Signal Books), 1962.

Zenos, Andrew C. Potiphar. In Jacobus, M. W., Lane, E. C., and Zenos, Andrew C. *Funk and Wagnalls new standard Bible dictionary.* Philadelphia: Blakiston, 1936.